SPIRITUALITY
IN DEPTH

Contents

Foreword

Murray Stein

THE WORK THAT GREAT SPIRITS DO LIVES AFTER THEM. IN FACT, IT increases in strength and influence. Irene Dugan was such a great spirit, and her work continues to grow and flourish in the world she so recently left behind. The essays in this book are a testimony to her ongoing presence, which as before is felt as a pressure to assume greater spiritual maturity, personal authority, and social responsibility.

The title chosen for this book of essays, "Spirituality in Depth," reflects Irene Dugan's understanding of her life's mission. As a spiritual director, she used methods that were designed to lead those who came to her for guidance deeper into their own inner centers. There they would experience a new kind of prayer, a dialogue with spiritual reality that inevitably challenged them to new insights and actions. To include spirituality with depth in one's life is, as Irene Dugan knew very well, to stay attuned to the Divine in every act undertaken and every plan or thought entertained. It is to live in constant communion with the invisible world that surrounds and embraces us.

This book is one more fruit on the tree planted and nourished by Irene Dugan in her long life of service, especially in her last years. The essays refer to her story with love and appreciation; they also contain seeds for further growth and developments. Irene's mind reached out constantly for a new future and for transformation of outworn modes and styles of thinking and believing. Ever the pioneer and innovator, Irene was impatient with the useless trappings of tradition for its own sake. Her mission was to deliver the good news of abundant life in the spirit to one and all, in whatever form was most effective and by whatever means spoke to the soul.

As a student of Jung and a friend of Ira Progoff, Irene knew the reality of the unconscious and the value of dreams. With one foot planted squarely in her Roman Catholic tradition and religious community, she ventured boldly forth with the other to explore the heights and plumb the depths of the psyche through her work with dreams, journals, and reflection. Dialogue was her method, and creative emergence of new insights was inevitably the result. People felt safe with her, and they went away knowing they were loved by a fierce and trustworthy friend. Her love was not always easy and comfortable, however, for confrontation and challenge were woven into its fabric. Irene sometimes scolded and chastised, but always it was done with the deepest respect and concern for the soul's ultimate well-being.

Irene was a teacher for whom teaching was life. Out of her mouth came many words of wisdom, but out of her eyes and her gestures and her actions flowed even greater teaching. She loved life, and all who came into contact with her "in depth" also came to love life and its author more than ever. May the same be said of those who pick up this book and read it.

Introduction

She's gone now,
and yet her spirit and
all the things with which she gifted me,
because they are things of the spirit,
continue all around me
like an aura and
within me like a fire.

—Dick Westley

THIS VOLUME OF ESSAYS IS DEDICATED TO SISTER IRENE DUGAN, A Religious of the Cenacle, a woman of fire. She's gone now from the dimension of consciousness in which we knew her, but because, as Dick Westley says, she was about the things of the spirit, she remains active in our auras and alive within us like a fire.

Irene Dugan was born in 1909 in New York City. In 1930, she entered the international Roman Catholic community of women known as the Religious of the Cenacle. The Cenacle sisters dedicate themselves to the ministries of spiritual care and companionship, teaching the art forms of prayer and interior growth and guiding souls through days of reflection and retreat experiences. Their name is biblically based in the post-resurrection and ascension narratives as the followers of Jesus struggle to discern the meaning of all the things that had gone on (Luke 24:13–35). The Books of Acts (1:12–14) records their gathering in the cenacle, or upper room, so that "with one accord they devoted themselves to prayer." The inspiration for the Sisters of the Cenacle's life of prayer, community, and service to the spiritual ministries springs from the first cenacle where the apostles and some women, including Mary, prayed in the *coenaculum* (cenacle) for the outpouring of the spirit promised by Jesus.

Irene Dugan professed her perpetual vows with the Religious of the Cenacle in 1938 when she was twenty-nine years old, and she remained a vibrant flame of faith, a firebrand to be reckoned with, burning with a quest for God to her death at eighty-seven in 1997. Irene Dugan had long been encouraged by her colleagues and friends to put in writing the legacy of her spiritual insight. After spending more than twenty years on it, she completed a manuscript only months before her death. Her book opens with a greeting: "I write these pages not for the learned or academic but for the seekers, flounderers, stargazers, and lovers, such as myself." Those who have contributed to this collection of essays in her honor count themselves among the seekers, flounderers, stargazers, and lovers who, through having known her, more generously savor the spiritual journey in depth.

The latter part of the twentieth century witnessed an international and interdisciplinary resurgence of interest in spirituality. Within the past two decades scholarly interest has focused on recovering the mystical traditions in the experience of religion with attention to spiritual growth, human social development, and psychological maturity. This is the arena of Sister Irene Dugan's most novel, artistic, intellectually and spiritually broadening work. In her spiritual mentoring, training of spiritual directors, and leadership in spiritual growth, Sister Dugan blended the traditions of Christian spirituality with modern depth psychology and the arts and, in her own way, pioneered what we may call depth spirituality.

The field of psycho-spiritual integration has its roots in the work of one of the founders of modern depth psychology, Carl Gustav Jung. Depth psychology attends to what lies beneath the surface of conscious awareness. It is a sacred science that examines the ways unconscious processes reveal themselves in symbol, dreams, images, art, and various biological and emotional symptoms. It is, in a sense, a spiritual tradition of its own because it relies upon and reverences the timeless legacies of literature, mythology, the arts, the panoply of holy books, and all forms of human creation and culture. These resources are brought to bear upon the quest to understand the human psyche and soul – the inner world and its workings – and to address the fragmenting problems of our time.

Irene's personal quest and interpersonal call to greater transparency and congruency in life suggests to us that she was like a prism. The authors in this text were part of the spectrum of light refracted by the prismatic Irene Dugan. The essays reflect a multifaceted array of perspectives, voice, and style, arising from different walks of life and professional experience. Yet each is an exercise in the artistry of depth spirituality learned from one who chose not to travel the usual way. As Jungian analyst Charles Asher says, "You can put many a fine point on the passion for the divine, but I have no doubt that Jung was madly and fiercely in love with God, scorched by the divine fire" (Slattery and Corbett 2000, p. 30). Sister Irene Dugan was an intimate of the fire of God. She ignited an unquenchable flame that spills over in the words you will find in these essays.

Mary Ann Bergfeld opens the text with a quote from Oliver Wendall Holmes: "Alas for those who never sing but die with all their music in them" – a counterpoint to Irene Dugan's endless curiosity for the new. Bergfeld offers a personal window into the "largeness" of Sister Dugan by reflecting on the expanse of their thirty-year friendship through the lens of their shared appreciation for the visual and performance arts. The essay is poetic and sobering as Bergfeld opines, "For those of us who have less gusto or courage for living 'large,' separation from access to the good and the beautiful will be less difficult." Bergfeld's essay sets the stage to more fully appreciate Sister Irene Dugan in her own words.

"Largesse Is Journey's End" is an excerpt from Sister Dugan's unpublished manuscript, completed only months before her death. She describes the labor that each person must experience in order to give birth to a deeper, freer self. She is a connoisseur of the examined life and her insights on psycho-spiritual transformation are part of her rich spiritual legacy. "Love," which for Dugan is the source and summit of the human and holy journey, "is all around in disguise."[1]

Murray Stein, in "The Reality of the Soul," creatively unravels the symbolic disguise of the transcendent breaking into human midst. Stein's provocative story of a butterfly – a manifestation of Irene's enduring presence – illustrates the synthesis of matter and spirit, offering the reader a window into the mystery of the soul. In his story, synchronicity upended his "habit of conscious doubt," and for a moment in time the veil that separates heaven and earth lifted. Those in the lifework of psychological practice, dream analysis, or spiritual counseling will find his insights into the meaning of symbol and the experience of transcendence wise and compelling.

Margaret Zulaski explores the symbolic world in "Dreams – The Hidden Treasures of the Unconscious." Zulaski names Irene Dugan spiritual director, mentor, and friend whose keen insight into a person's hidden potential evokes trust in the activity of one's inner life. Dreams catch the divine at work by revealing the underlying meaning of life and therefore of God. According to Jung, dreams are not about the verifiable dimensions of our actual lives. Dreams carry our questions and our difficulties. We dream the solutions we cannot grasp in conscious life. Our dreams are exceedingly valuable, as Jung reminds, precisely because they cannot cheat. Meshing depth psychological insight into dreams and individuation with the fundamental convictions of incarnational spirituality, Zulaski shows us how to uncover aspects of our individual destiny in dreams and to gain richer access to the God within.

The next two essays explain and explore two depth spiritual dispositions that assist the seeker and flounderer in the search for freedom. Jane Madejczyk simply and subtly suggests that spiritual detachment is an art form that, when achieved, permits a "love for life" unknown by those whose lives are riddled with the urgencies of material consumption and success. This, Madejczck reports, she learned through a zesty friendship with Irene Dugan, who "could listen to an excuse once but set a blue-eyed glare flashing if it showed up again." Relating the theories of depth psychology to the sayings of Jesus and Buddhist monk Thich Nhat Hanh, Madejczyk explores how inner work and heightened awareness for "loving life" surprisingly led her to the conclusion that true "understanding leads to detachment and detachment leads to love."

In a similar vein, Michael Cooper traces the roots of "a spirituality of balance" in the teachings of Jesus, the community spirituality of St. Benedict, the discernments of spirits of St. Ignatius of Loyola, and dream work and the midlife journey in Jungian psychology. In preparing his essay, Cooper commented, "In taking a prayerful regard over the twenty-five plus years of friendship, what stands out for me is Sister Irene's deeply contemplative spirit of balance." For those desiring to know this contemplative spirit, Cooper searches the inner terrain of a spirituality of balance in all things and all manner of living. Dugan and Cooper shared a love for the spiritual exercises of Ignatius, the founder of the Society of Jesus and a guiding influence in the spiritual formation of the Religious of the Cenacle. Cooper quotes Jesuit Teilhard de Chardin in offering a commentary on a spirituality of balance in *all* things: "Nothing is profane for those who have eyes to see."

Joyce Kemp, a Religious of the Cenacle, credits her sister Irene with introducing her to the Intensive Journal process of Dr. Ira Progoff. In "The Discernment of Life Tasks in the Progoff Intensive Journal Process," Kemp presents the reader with an overview of the classic spiritual growth tools pioneered by Dr. Ira Progoff. Sister Irene Dugan gave Dr. Progoff his introduction to the Midwest by inviting him in 1972 to begin offering Intensive Journal workshops through the Cenacles in the Midwest. Progoff believed, according to Kemp, that "healing comes from going inward and bringing to the surface our deepest heart's desire." She details how the Intensive Journal process enables a person to go into his or her depths and discover the "seed-images" of unlived potential. An Intensive Journal consultant, Kemp carefully guides the reader through Progoff's work and the unique features and methods that direct, aid, deepen, and bring to awareness personal potentials seeking expression. As Kemp says, "the next step we are to take in life is the one that has presented itself to us intuitively from the depths of our being."

Over twenty years ago, through the mediation of Sister Irene Dugan, Avis Clendenen had the singular privilege of reading Ira Progoff's never-published manuscript, "Moses and God." This was Clendenen's first foray into the application of the insights of depth psychology to biblical figures and wisdom. In "No Shortcuts to the Promised Land: Creating Character from Crises," Clendenen analyses the biblical story of Moses as a paradigm for psycho-spiritual becoming. For Clendenen, Moses' journey to consciousness, forged through crises, tells the tale of our potential, women and men alike, to hear the blazing Voice that calls us each by name.

Four years before Irene Dugan died, Dick Westley interviewed her for a pastoral newsletter on the topic of evil. Since the audience of the newsletter was primarily Catholic parish ministers, Irene decided to say a few words about the operation of authority in the Church. She said, "Evil in the Church arises from authoritarianism, not true 'authority,' which is *ab audire* – I move from what I hear within me, and it is the truth which speaks to me . . . So *when I move from the truth that is in me I hurt no one – but I scare the whole world.*" "Giving up the

Faith – In Order to Be Faithful" is Dick Westley's invigorating and bold design for abandoning a religion of childhood and facing the scary challenges of adult faith. He takes with serious delight the Pauline admonition: "When I was a child I used to talk like a child, think like a child, reason like a child. When I became a man I put childish ways aside" (1 Cor. 13: 11). Westley's thesis is found in his conviction that people are not giving up on faith in order to run from God or their spiritual responsibilities, rather they are exercising their authority in order to be more faithful to the God of their experience and the reality of their responsibilities in a diverse and pluralistic world. In a philosophical theologian's logic, he outlines six "unbelievables" that must be abandoned for the Church to be a place where one can thrive as an adult child of God.

Robert J. Bueter continues in this stream in "Living the Spiritual Life with Authority." Bueter has been long intrigued by Sister Irene Dugan's "magisterial manner" and "good authority." Following Westley, he offers a fresh and cogent analysis of the *ad intra* and *ad extra* challenges to the magisterial church and the faithful prompted by the current "culture wars." Bueter attempts a path across the contentious divide to suggest a perspective on authority that is not one of argument or accusation but one of meditation and mediation anchored in and measured by the gospel of Jesus.

The final essay, "From Generation to Generation: Passing on a Legacy of Hope" by Bruce Wellems, brings Irene Dugan's story full circle by telling the story of her final ministerial horizon: working with adolescent boys and girls struggling in gangs and surrounded by violence. Wellems opens his essay in 1996 recounting Irene's once-a-month meetings with a group of young men fourteen to nineteen years of age. She guided these youths at risk in learning a process of life skills reflection that would help them find the inner resources to combat the lure of gangs and the consequent school failure and life of violence. Wellems records that "the eighty-seven-year-old nun was direct, sincere, and loving with these young men. . . . One seventeen-year-old was asked, after a session, why he listened to Irene, and he said simply, 'She has authority.'" Establishing a basis of mutual respect created a milieu of openness, trust, and willingness to let "an old nun" be a voice of loving authority to a small band of street smart, poor, tough, and frightened teenage boys. Wellems was their pastor, and he had feared they were lost until Irene said bring them to her. Thus, the small monthly reflection group meetings gave birth, one year after Irene's death, to the opening of the Sister Irene Dugan Alternative Public High School, located in the Back of the Yards neighborhood on the near southwest side of Chicago. Wellem's inspirational essay will leave the reader in a spirit of *magnificat*, reveling in blessed possibilities of hope generation unto generation.

My hope is that the reader may encounter the spirit of Sister Irene Dugan as a prism whose colorful and multifaceted life continues to prompt interest in the inner terrain of depth spirituality. I am deeply grateful to each of the authors who honored Sister Irene Dugan through their dedicated and creative efforts to contribute to this *festschrift* text. Without the generous assistance of Irene's dear friend Barbara Howard and the Howard Family Foundation, I would never have been able to claim the time to animate and orchestrate this project. I am indebted to the Religious of the Cenacle of the North American Province for the trust placed in me to respect, preserve, and perpetuate their sister Irene's rich spiritual legacy. It was Murray Stein who believed from the beginning that such a book, inspired by the indomitable spirit of Sister Irene Dugan, r.c., would be appreciated by the wider audience of those interested in the intersection of depth psychology and spirituality. Without his encouragement and support, our work would not be taking its place on the list of Chiron Publications. From the moment the manuscript was placed in the hands of Siobhan Drummond, our words took new wings. Her skill as a wordsmith, crafter of good writing and visual design, has invaluably enhanced the artistry of the book. And finally, it was Mary Ann Bergfeld, RSM, who first introduced me to Irene Dugan when I was twenty-one years old and it has been her company and conversations these past years since Irene's death that provided the gusto and courage to take seriously the inheritance.

May all who strive to live spirituality in depth celebrate the promise that we need not die with all the music in us.

Avis Clendenen
January 2001

Note

1. *Love Is All Around in Disguise: Meditations for Spiritual Seekers* is the title of Irene Dugan's book, being prepared for publication by Avis Clendenen.

Reference

Slattery, D., and L. Corbett. 2000. *Depth Psychology: Meditations in the Field.* Einsiedeln: Daimon Verlag.

Significant Dates in the Life of Sister Irene Dugan, r.c.

December 4, 1909	Born in New York City, the eldest of nine children of Thomas Dugan and Irene McBride Dugan
September 8, 1930	Entered the Religious of the Cenacle in Lake Ronkonkoma, New York
June 2, 1938	Perpetual profession of vows
September 1938	Ministry at the Cenacle in Boston
June 1943	One of the founders of the Cenacle in Milwaukee, Wisconsin
January 1956	Ministry at the Carmichael Cenacle in Sacramento, California
February 1963	Ministry at the Longwood Cenacle in Chicago
1970	Began training and giving Progoff Intensive Journal workshops in the United States and Europe
1973	Founded with Paul Robb, SJ, the Spiritual Direction Institute in collaboration with the Jesuit School of Theology in Chicago
	Appointed adjunct faculty in spiritual direction training at the Jesuit School of Theology in Chicago
1981	Sabbatical in LaLouvesc, France, birthplace of the Congregation of the Cenacle
1983	Appointed scholar in residence at the Institute of Pastoral Studies, Loyola University, Chicago
1987	Doctor of Humane Letters, *honoris causa*, from Loyola University, Chicago
1988	Resided at the Fullerton Cenacle in Chicago and continued to write and teach
1996	Began ministry with local youth from the Chicago area
July 21, 1997	Died in Chicago
August 25, 1998	The Sister Irene Dugan Alternative Public High School opened in Chicago for youth at risk

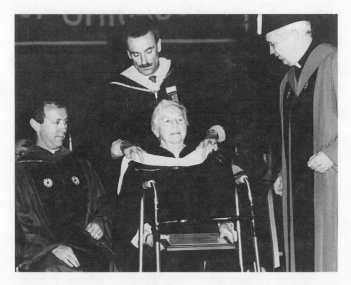

Sister Irene Dugan, r.c., receiving Doctor of Humane Letters, *honoris causa*, from Loyola University, Chicago, 1987. *From left*: Dr. Timothy O'Connell, Director, Institute of Pastoral Studies; George Hostert; Sister Irene Dugan, r.c.; Rev. Raymond Baumhart, SJ, President.

Irene Dugan –
Her Life Was a Song

᭡

Mary Ann Bergfeld, RSM

Alas for those who never sing but die with all their music in them.

—Oliver Wendell Holmes

THE LATE 1960S AND THE 1970S WERE AN EXHILARATING TIME FOR lovers of ideas, especially for ideas coming from a Europe reviving from and reflecting on its experience of World War II. But most exciting to those who were eager for such insights was the fact that these ideas were being carried in the universal language of film, and European films were at last available to American audiences.

In the 1950s, the Supreme Court made two landmark decisions that impacted Americans' "access to ideas." The Paramount case broke Hollywood's monopoly on film distribution to theaters in America.[1] *The Miracle* case was the test case for film censorship.[2] The Court acknowledged films as a carrier of ideas and as such protected by the first and fourteenth amendments, which guaranteed freedom of speech to motion pictures for the first time.

It was in this climate that I first came to know and value Irene Dugan. Her habit, as I came to know, was to be open and inquiring about all in high and popular culture that was impacting those she counseled or taught. I was recently home from film school, preoccupied with the technical and artistic achievements of this art form that I love. Through the Screen Educators' Society I met Irene; I was never again allowed to critique a film's artistic achievement separate from its ideas. We began early on to debate the interaction of meaning and presentation of Bergman's existentialism, Roemer's moral debates, and

Kurosawa's Eastern aesthetic. The whole world of ideas was ours for investigation, and what fun we had.

At this time I had no idea how Irene's experience at La Louvesc, France, had influenced her. I think that European experience broadened her and created in her a desire to explore a wider world than had been part of her family or Cenacle development. Until she became physically incapacitated and could no longer travel, Europe with its diversity and complexity continued to draw her and to inform her thought.

So we explored that world through film. Very few foreign films made their way south of the Chicago Loop in those days, so our adventures usually involved trips from southside Chicago to downtown or its environs. These trips became occasions for extended conversations and vigorous debates on the meanings of the latest film experience. They also became the basis for explorations of larger topics.

Irene's knowledge of and sensitivity to the spiritual dimensions of the human experience informed and tempered my inexperience. Antonioni's rendering of the nature of evil and human irresponsibility in *Blowup* led to questions about sin, evil, and personal responsibility. Mira Nair's *Salaam Bombay* took us to places we had never been and provoked talk of a suffering we in America had never known. Mike Nichol's *Who's Afraid of Virginia Woolf?* forced us to debate the nature of physical and verbal violence. Kei Kuimai's *Sandakan 8* broke our hearts and gave us new insights into compassion. Our moviegoing became more than entertainment or an academic pursuit. It became the basis of a firm friendship.

Debates about meanings carried in the world of fiction led us to discussions about happenings in the world we inhabited as religious women. Here, too, the world was changing. Vatican II had caused a chasm in religious life as we had known it. A Catholicism that had condemned modernism in 1907 and that had too frequently flirted with Jansenism now reached out under Pope John XXIII to embrace Teilhard de Chardin's vision: "By virtue of the Creation, and still more of the Incarnation, nothing here below is profane for those who know how to see."

I am convinced that Irene's appreciation for the beautiful and the good was rooted in this conviction. And how she loved life and all creation. And how freely! Visits with her were conducted over crusty bread and sweet butter that was savored with joy. I have always believed that enthusiasm over Itami's *Tampopo* or Gabriel Axel's *Babette's Feast* was more visceral than rational. Exchanges with Irene might include a reference to a favorite opera, an inspirational book, a theater piece she'd heard or read about. You could expect an evening phone call if some special television program shouldn't be missed. She saved and annotated the "Arts and Leisure" and "Review of Books" sections of the Sunday *New York Times* for friends.

These exchanges were the coin of her friendship; and no one had a greater capacity for friendship. No one kept better care for your loved ones; no one knew as exactly the vulnerabilities you hid. And no one had greater expectations of you than she. You were expected to care as deeply about the development of her students and those in her spiritual direction as she did. What was available that would help them understand suffering? How could they be brought to embrace this good, God-created universe instead of seeing it as tainted or threatening? What experiences could be provided that could help them reconcile their frequently confusing and often harsh experience of the institutional Church? She cared deeply about all of creation – but most especially for those who became her special responsibility. I think one of the greatest lessons of her teaching was her openness to possibilities.

It was during one of our conversations about the changing role of religious in the Church that I shared with Irene a concern I had about a Saint Xavier student I was driving to school every morning. This theology student, seriously considering religious life, had been told to find a spiritual director. My indignation about placing that expectation on an inexperienced young woman prompted a typical Irene-ism: "Bring her to me." And so I brought young Avis Clendenen to the Longwood Cenacle to meet Sister Irene Dugan. It proved to be a fortuitous meeting.

The last days of our friendship ended in much the same way they had begun – taking vicarious pleasure in the ideas and adventures brought to us through the film experience. But life on the big screen was now reduced to the infinitely smaller and less satisfying video experience. Savoring a special meal was now dependent on the special kindness of a friend who made all the arrangements, including travel in a medicar. The joy of a special occasion carried with it the awareness of temporal and physical limitations.

In truth, our last conversations were silent exchanges; years of friendship had tutored us to each other's thoughts. We both knew what the loss of independence and of influence cost. For those of us who have less gusto or courage for living "large," separation from access to the good and the beautiful will be less difficult.

Irene's last lessons were painful to observe. It had been easier to talk about the meaning of Kurosawa's elegies on death and old age, *Ikiru* or *Rhapsody in August,* than it was now to live them. I don't think Irene ever really experienced "old"; happily, while her body had begun to fail, her mind remained clear and active. Her curiosity about what was new continued even as incapacity relegated her to the company of those for whom "the immediate" was no longer significant.

Rational conversations on reconciling relationships prompted by Ingmar Bergman's *Autumn Sonata* or *Cries and Whispers,* once satisfying, now became challenging. It was much easier to academically debate the pain caused by loss of independence in John Sayles's *Passion Fish* or loss of significance as presented in Bertolucci's *The Last Emperor* than to watch it lived out. For a woman long accustomed to exerting influence and initiating action, the inability to affect the direction of a ministry experiencing the challenge of declining numbers and new directions was wrenching. And Irene never had the gift of resignation.

James Ivory's elegant *Remains of the Day* continued to confront each of us about opportunities lost or decisions regretted. Her plans and actions that challenged the traditions of the Cenacle she loved were initiated and implemented with the expectation that they would prove a new good, but they were, I think, sometimes rued.

But Irene would never be burdened with the regrets Oliver Wendell Holmes lyrically posed: "Alas for those who never sing but die with all their music in them." Irene hymned for many of us, songs of war, chants of celebration, and of lament. Music that stays with us. I will be forever grateful for her early and last lessons to me. But it was a hard school that shaped her. I remain a student of her legacy.

Notes

1. *U.S. v. Paramount Pictures Inc.* was argued before the U.S. Supreme Court in October 1947. In May 1948 the Court ruled that the major Hollywood studios violated federal antitrust laws by monopolizing trade through their control of film distribution to theaters in the United States. The Court demand that studios divest themselves of their theater outlets opened the doors for independent and foreign film distribution in this country.

2. *Joseph Burstyn, Inc. v. Wilson* was argued before the U.S. Supreme Court in February 1952. The case charged Rossellini's *The Miracle* with "sacrilege." The Court declared that "it cannot be doubted that motion pictures are a significant medium for communication of ideas … and as such are within the free speech and free press guarantees of the First and Fourteenth Amendments." This grant of freedom of expression to motion pictures encouraged and allowed the importation and display of foreign films previously unavailable to American audiences.

Largesse Is Journey's End

❀

Irene Dugan, r.c., with Avis Clendenen

Introduction

SISTER IRENE DUGAN, R.C., COMPLETED THE FIRST SUBSTANTIAL draft of a manuscript entitled "Love Is All Around: In Disguise" only six weeks prior to her death in July 1997. A few weeks before her death, Irene and I had what would be our last conversation. She directed me to pick up a box that she left for me at the front desk at the Fullerton Cenacle. She did not mention that the box contained two copies of her manuscript, the computer disks, and all the notes related to her book. She was more interested in summing up our years of knowing one another and "directing" me in what she wanted for her funeral. She seemed in relatively good spirits and at one point was gazing quietly out her bedroom window with her back to me. As she was pondering she said to me, "Write this down. Are you listening? I know what I want on my memorial card." I said, "Go ahead, I'm ready." Irene proceeded, "I want my card to read, Wafted into Life, December 4, 1909…." Before she could go any further, I blurted out, "Wafted?" Swinging her wheelchair around to face me, looking simultaneously annoyed and amused, she spelled, "W A F T E D. Look it up."

I did look it up. According to the dictionary, *wafted* means "to be carried lightly and smoothly into the air or over water, to float or be carried in a current or even a gust." The word has the same root as another word meaning "an escort vessel," and it is, as well, related to the word meaning "a watchman or watchwoman." Irene Dugan was indeed wafted in life, savoring life as a gift over time, trial, and triumph. She floated back and forth and in and out of the lives of those who sought her counsel, at times a gentle breeze, at other times gusting boldly, but always the watchful escort vessel guiding others on their journey to freedom, wholeness, and deeper realms of love.

The cardboard box waiting for me at the Cenacle was a treasure chest filled with the written words of Sister Irene Dugan, r.c. This essay is of Irene's making, and I am simply the scribe wafting her words onto these pages.

"Love Is All Around: In Disguise" opens with this greeting from Irene: "I write these pages not for the learned or academic but for the seekers, flounderers, stargazers, and lovers, such as myself." She goes on to say:

> My friends, folks in class, and others have been after me for years to write a book. They keep saying, "Irene, you can't die unless you leave something for us." I couldn't understand what they were talking about and figured if I was giving them anything, surely it was the giving of myself every single day. In spite of this objection, the words kept coming, "Write a book! Write a book!" About ten years ago, I started to write about Ignatius of Loyola and Ira Progoff, two men who are very important to me. Ignatius was a sixteenth-century Spaniard whose spiritual conversion resulted in the founding of the Society of Jesus (Jesuits) and the creation of the inner journey known as the Spiritual Exercises.[1] Ira Progoff, a contemporary colleague and friend, is a depth psychologist and originator of the *Intensive Journal, At a Journal Workshop,* and Process Meditation™. While five centuries apart, Ignatius could have been a twentieth-century psychologist and Ira a sixteenth-century visionary. My original hope had been to attempt to integrate their ideas and teachings, going deeper and discovering more meaning. My first attempt failed for various reasons.
>
> I trust this effort, however, will reach completion. My book is an exercise in the disciplines of psychology and spirituality, an invitation to a journey toward self-knowledge. The tools of depth psychology and Christian spirituality can help anyone who wishes to enter the process of striving towards wholeness and holiness. The process is rigorous, freeing, and rewarding, all in one. It is an awesome process full of ups and downs, light and shadow, the known and unknowns, safety and risks. The objective is to free us gradually to be unafraid to look at the

experiences of our life, our inner and outer environments, and decide to walk the path of enlightenment and transformation.

With these words Irene Dugan began her *tour de force*. The following is a lengthy excerpt from chapter 6 of "Love Is All Around: In Disguise," where Irene explores her vision of spiritual transformation.[2]

Love, the Transformer

Ignatius calls the bookend of the Spiritual Exercise *"Contemplation Ad Amorem,"* translated "Contemplation to Obtain Love." In Spanish, the native language of Ignatius, it is *Contemplacion para alcanzar Amor,* meaning, "To anticipate the dawning of Love." From my vantage point, love is the mystery of care, of life, of production, and continuity of life passed from one human to another through the dynamic life of the Holy Trinity.

Love is a gathering together within the temple of our being all our energy and dynamism to apprehend love. Love is the most needed, least understood and heeded of human necessities. Love is an unparalleled gift that is too often avoided, even discarded.

We speak of a "labor of love" or of "love's labor lost" with stress on the word *love,* and pass over the prime word *labor.* Labor has the flavor of creating, preserving, and developing something, something we have inherently, and so is an incessant knocking for our attention and response. God does this to perfection, laboring over their handiwork.[3] We are invited and required to enter into their labor in order to shape ourselves under their tutelage, to their image. Through this mutuality, we take on the world, the cosmos, and love it to maturity.

And so we arrive at a deep attentive consciousness that knows "in my end is my beginning, and in my beginning is my end." Such unity is endlessly desired and so seldom entered into because it is under our noses, and our noses have lost their sense of smell due to inner and outer smog. We need to come into our senses sharply and brightly so that we see freshly, hear acutely, touch tenderly, taste with relish, and take time metaphorically and literally to "smell the flowers."

> *[God] has showed you, O [humans] what is good;*
> *and what does the Lord require of you*

but to do justice, and to love kindness,
and to walk humbly with your God?

(Micah 6:8)

We are made sensuous beings, and reclaiming this gift is an art to be cultivated or we shall not be grasped by love. Love is a pure, sensuous gift assuring me,

> I never was alone. I never am alone. I never will be alone, even if I dis-own the Presence. The automatic drive in me moves to constant self-awareness, self-alertness, self-development, and self-arrival. This faces me head-on to the Other, out of whom I spring, am shaped and formed, and a transforming union is experienced. This is my end and my beginning. (Buber 1996, p. 3)

In this day and age, my beingness and ability to come to Other springs from my daily experience of traveling through layers of accumulated artifacts of the self, to the cleansing waters and mirroring love of the Begetting Being.

Interaction of Lover and Beloved

Mutuality mediates transformation. Yet transformation, as a process of growth, relies most often on the ordinary formative developments of our lives. Formation begins in the womb of our mother, continues under family influence through infancy and early preschool years (though now, in the almost twenty-first century, due to the pressures of both parents working and the consequent explosion of child-care options, such family-based formation is not a given). The next stage, school or its equivalent, makes a strong imprint on children. The experience of schooling has a definitive and defining impact on formation. This is followed in great intensity by entry into the demands of professional life and the many choices of avocations. We can be drugged by the lure of billboards, super sales techniques, and an unexamined grasping nature. We are shaped, reshaped, and misshaped through the unique features of our developmental process. At long last, if we are alive and alert, we begin to listen to our own life suggesting that it is time for us to take our formation into our own hands. This inaugurates a major transitional phase urging us to consider profound decision-making about how we are going to live *now*.

Consciously examining the imprint of external authority on our lives, we gradually begin to take back the power over ourselves that we had given away and never acknowledged. The dumping/blaming syndrome comes to a grinding halt as I am confronted with the self, saying, "Now I begin ... Begin? Begin what?" Re-formation! It is my turn to form, shape, and mold the product that is uniquely me according to the inner work at hand. A first question might be, "What is at hand?" Then follows the inventory of what it is at hand, meaning the native resources within myself, out of which I gradually create the SELF waiting to be born. Previously unobserved doors, windows, caverns, and heights emerge before me. Looking at them makes me shudder until I slowly quiet down and let my inner voice speak, listening to love's lure and its direction. My life's journey shifts and the process of mature transformation is summoned into reality.

All creation has been awaiting this swell of the movement of love towards Love. Transformation, as an endemic force in the press toward wholeness, while painful, demands an active give-over to love. The childish and adolescent exertions of egomania, fixations on what others think, and solely seeking external approvals loses its power and is replaced by an inner drive digging deeper into the essence of who I am and who I desire to be. The Psalmist sings, "Sacrifice and offering you do not desire; but you have given me ears that *dig after you*" (Psalm 40:6 Revised Standard Version). Reliance on the virtues of trust and fidelity create the inner condition that enables the journey to deeper regions of my being and taps the essential fundamentals of transformation. I become immune to the sirens of possession, hoarding, and, above all, success and its allurements. Wavering at this juncture of human becoming can spell disaster, serious wavering, that is, which carries the flavor of fearing the truth of spiritual adulthood.

The terrain is rugged, the riverbed not quite even, and so we fight and flow with the currents. Doubts that we are on the right way fly hither and thither in an attempt to erode trust and fidelity. Our beliefs are redefined from the inner out. The dross is burned away and the gold of love – the embrace of the sacrality and mutuality of our lives – begins to shine through. The moments when we are conscious of changing or having been changed are mighty moments. It is as if we *see* Love as a pillar of cloud by day and one of fire by night (Exodus 13:21-22 RSV). The trust was worth the trusting; the faithfulness to the way, a journey to the promised land. The state of transformation is rich with spiritual paradox: we live in an atmosphere of quietude and calm and, at the same time, of extraordinary activity surrounding the *kairos* of our becoming a new creation (II Corinthians 5:17 RSV).

My will has now become supple and attentive to the voice of the Beloved, from whom I now hear the Voice within. At this level of intentional living and holy relationship, flexibility and fluidity of movement are reinforced. I am in union and harmony with Love. My whole being is infused with this awareness, and my desire is never to be separated from its passion.

> *THOU SHALT KNOW [GOD] WHEN [GOD] COMES*
> *Not by any din of drums—*
> *Not by the vantage of [any] airs—*
> *Not by anything [God] wears—*
> *Nor [any] gown—*
>
> *FOR [GOD'S] PRESENCE KNOWN SHALL BE*
> *By the Holy Harmony*
> *That [God's] coming makes in thee—*
>
> (unknown fifteenth-century writer)

Nestled in Holy Harmony is a mysteriously dynamic relationship. Transformation is mediated by this mutuality and has its entitlements and obligations, as any truly authentic and significant relationship. Life with the Beloved is strenuous because it involves the living out of the receiving and the giving of love. Attentive alertness to the Presence is imperative. Alert listening and hearing – activation of these inner senses – become second nature as the transforming process bears fruit. I live in tandem with creation and creativity, the music of the spheres envelops me as I become a living God to the world, the universe, the cosmos. A craving for simplicity in living and its consequent freedom reigns. Clinging to the old self falls away. I experience a sense of my inner environment as uncluttered and ordered. Love flows through me and neutralizes all disintegrative and destructive evil forces. Paul in his letter to the Galatians put it this way, "I live now not with my own life but with the life of Christ who lives in me" (Gal. 2:20 New Jerusalem Bible). This is a season of alertness and inner brightness. Energy is neither blocked nor wasted. True life flows and is shared as love requires, and the lifeline is thus kept open for the free exchange of giving and receiving love. The process is simultaneously elevating and devastating.

> Rabbi Moshe Leib of Sassov said: "How to love [people] is something I learned from a peasant who was sitting in an inn with other peasants, drinking. For a long time he was as silent as all the rest, but when he was moved by the wine, he asked one of the men seated beside him: 'Tell me, do you love me or don't you love me?' The other replied: 'I love you very much.' But the first peasant replied: 'You say that you love me, but do you know what I need? If you really loved me you would know.' The other had not a word to say to this, and the peasant who had put the question fell silent again. But I understood. To know the needs of men and women and to bear the burden of their sorrow – this is true love." (Buber 1996, p. 2)

Largesse Is Journey's End

Love opens our eyes, hearts, and hands in wide embrace of the all of life. An aura of eternity marks the season where largesse is Journey's End. The temporal has found its place and is the bridge to the other shore, also known as heaven. Heaven is an idea we tend to leave alone, bypass, or sigh over. We seem to fear swirling it around in a brandy snifter for taste, lest it evaporate, leaving us with nothing but the vapors. Yet, heaven does not ask us to address it, familiarize ourselves with it, so that we end up yearning for it with great intensity. For that to occur, we must devote time for savoring its mystery.

What do you feel, what do you think heaven to be like? St. Paul had this to say: "Of this wisdom it is written: Eye has not seen, ear has not heard, nor has it so much as dawned on [humans] what God has prepared for those who love [God]" (1 Cor. 2:9 New American Bible). When we are fully alive, alert, and aware here on earth, we are full of energy to explore, discover, and dig out every possible area of learning and experiencing the knowledge and wisdom at our fingertips. The excitement of increased knowledge and understanding through experience impels us into further searching, even when extra energy and push are necessary.

Heaven is going to be all this excitement, plus more, without the darkness and the disappointment that is inherent during our earthly pilgrimage. Boredom apparently is not a trait in God's being. Ergo, boredom ceases to exist in the largesse that is Journey's End. We will never live long enough to be satiated with respect to all the beauties and burdens of life. Music, science, literature, all areas of art, including culinary arts, are endless vistas open to our searching and inquisitive nature, to be pursued with pleasure, ease, and excitement. The challenges, enormous sorrows, and profound sufferings are but guises for growth. The God who stands by our side in times of struggle – always knowing our need and bearing our burden – is the same God who beckons us to the Divine household at journey's end where we reside forever in our natural dwelling place.

The gateway to this bliss is death, which turns out to be a friend rather than a foe. Death is the doorway of final transformation into unending life, light, and love. Death, then, as well as love, is the Transformer. Henri Nouwen writes,

> Dying is the most general human event, something we all have to do. But do we do it well? Is our death more than an unavoidable fate that we simply wish would not be? Can it somehow become an act of fulfillment, perhaps more human than any other act?
>
> . . . When we contemplate with compassion the suffering and pain both around the world and close to home, we receive a gift: a reminder of the "great human sameness" of "all of us [who] will die and participate in the same end." When we offer companionship to the dying we remember and celebrate the lives of the departed, we create a reciprocal "community of care" and "remind each other that we will bear fruit beyond the few years we have to live." . . . When we face death with hope we make the choice of faith, a choice based on the conviction that we see not only failure on the cross of Jesus, but victory as well, not only destruction, but new life as well, not only nakedness but glory as well. (Nouwen 1994, p. XIV)

There is no satiety in heaven, only largesse. We experience the wholeness of creation and our own as well, for all will be ours forever in freedom. Yet this experience is devoid of acquisitiveness to possess, dominate, or manipulate. All is healed, the human and divine mingle and become one. In this dimension of new being there is no need to believe because we shall have vision. We shall see God face-to-face and bask in knowledge of the true Paternity/Maternity. Hope will be absorbed in the final embrace of the God of our yearning. What will remain is love – love as we never imagined could be experienced as real. The totality of living is ours in sheer wonder and joy. Why, then, are we so shy about contemplating this reality?

Each of us will be transformed. Each of us will be a new creation and yet remain our true self without impediments. We will go to the depth of the sea and explore its treasures without scuba diving equipment. We will fly to Uranus without space ships. We will plumb the deep recesses of humanness, and our largesse to embrace the discovery will be limitless. We will roam with dinosaurs, understand and converse in all languages and no language. We will sing arias and folk songs in praise of God. We will experience what it actually means to be an heir of God. The divine will shine in and through us, and it will be only the beginning. We shall be complete human beings in a continuing movement of union.

When I dream of heaven, I experience a feeling of excitement that what I am doing now is made more worthwhile by the vision of what is to come. Therefore, it is the now that intimates what will be. Therefore, I want to be related to and involved in the now of my existence and not consumed by fear or searching for baubles and commodities that erode and fade. I am the custodian of my soul, whose life is guided by the Master Crafter.

I am universal, in that all that ever was exists in me. I am a song of the Universe with all the chords of creation played out in me. Such is the optimism of one who lives an examined life. Love is all around in the disguise of now. *"The unexamined life is not worth living"*

Conclusion: Dying in Character

Thus Irene ends her extended reflection on the art form of spiritual transformation, the largesse of eternity, and the possibility and promise of living the now. Wafted into life in 1909, she gusted about for eighty-seven abundantly rich years on this side of eternity. For many of us, she was an escort vessel, gently yet "persuasively" guiding our journey, always a watchwoman of some larger vision. The full measure of her contribution to transformational spirituality lies hidden in the hearts of the thousands of persons she companioned along the marvelously treacherous pilgrimage we call life.

Literally hours before her death on July 21, 1997, Irene's nurse was prepared to give her an injection for pain. It was reported to me that Irene gestured for the nurse to stop. She knew that the medication would make her less conscious, less viscerally aware. True to character, she indicated her desire not to be sedated away from the now of her dying by simply saying, "No, please, I want to have the experience." And so she did. And so she is experiencing the largesse at journey's end that some day will be our now.

Notes

1. The Spiritual Exercises of St. Ignatius of Loyola – detailed practices for spiritual deepening – is a classic of Christian spirituality. Composed by Ignatius between 1533 and 1541, the work contains instructions, admonitions, annotations, examinations, warnings, prayers, meditations, and other exercises aimed at leading one to virtue, discernment of spirits, renewal in faith, and transformation through love; a detailed "four-week process" for conversion.

2. Avis Clendenen is completing Sister Irene Dugan's book under the title "Love Is All Around in Disguise: Meditations for Spiritual Seekers."

3. Sister Dugan understood God's dynamic nature as essentially Trinitarian. She often made reference to Genesis 1:26, "Then God said, 'Let *us* make humankind in *our* own image, after *our* likeness . . . .'" Plurality in God is critical to fully understanding the theological framework that informed Sister Dugan's life work in spiritual direction. The Christian doctrine of the Trinity, always mysteriously confounding, might be best expressed as one God with three ways of being: (1) as Unconditional Love, *agape;* (2) incarnate and Incarnational, Word-made-flesh; and (3) Life Source within the depth of each human spirit, Ground of faith and hope gifting each for others, Animator of community. In sum, we experience God as one, yet as having three distinguishable ways of being.

References

Buber, M. 1996. *Ministry of Money.* Newsletter, no. 103 (August).

Nouwen, H. 1994. *Our Greatest Gift: A Meditation on Dying and Caring.* New York: Harper Collins.

The Reality of the Soul

Murray Stein

"[T]he unconscious tends to regard spirit and matter not merely as equivalent but as actually identical . . . ."

Jung, "A Study in the Process of Individuation"

ARRIVING FAR TOO EARLY TO DELIVER A LECTURE ONE SUNDAY morning, I decided to go outside and pass the time walking in the warm sunshine. It was a bright sunny day in Arizona, and I was pleased to be spending a few days away from a freezing Chicago in February. I agreed with my hosts to return at 10:15, since the meeting would begin at 10:30. Wandering around the pleasant park adjacent to the meeting place, I concentrated on the points I wanted to make in my talk. It was a quiet place, and I quickly became deeply absorbed in thought and completely lost track of the time.

Suddenly I was startled from my reverie by a sharp birdcall directly behind me. It was an unusual sound, difficult to ignore and unlike any bird's song I had heard before. It pierced right through my cocoon of unconsciousness and arrested my thoughts, as though directed specifically to me. The little bird was trying to get my attention, or so it felt. Am I in a fairy tale? I wondered half consciously.

The bird whistled three times and then flew to another tree just ahead of me as though leading me forward. It called again. By now I was fully awake, and it occurred to me to check the time. I looked down at my watch and saw that it was exactly 10:15. The birdcall had kept me on schedule. I could have missed the meeting. This was nature's own alarm clock!

For the natural people of the world, this type of experience – when animals genuinely speak to them and offer greater consciousness—is expected. Also for students of myth and fairy tales the helpful animal is commonplace. In Wagner's opera *Siegfried,* for instance, a little bird leads the hero on his journey. In the bible, Balaam's ass sees the angel and saves the ignorant man's life. But to the sophisticated and highly technological people of Western modern (and postmodern) consciousness, this type of experience seems incredible. We have erected an impenetrable wall between human consciousness and the rest of the natural world. To overcome this artificial barrier – to climb over it, to transcend it – we need to experience symbols that join these seeming opposites into a unified whole.

The little bird in Arizona was such a symbol.

There are certain special moments in life – I call them "openings to transcendence" – when we confront a symbol and see reality as the unconscious regards it all the time. At this level, the psyche knows no difference between spirit and matter. They are identical. Figures from both dimensions of reality are experienced as woven of the same threads. Human thoughts and the song of birds are parts of a single fabric.

I am speaking of the transcendence of the psyche, the reality of the soul. People have had experiences of the soul's transcendence since time immemorial. Yet we continue to wonder, What do they prove? Do such experiences offer a genuine vision of reality, or are they only products of human imagination? Are they rooted in human desire, in the wish for immortality, in projection? Was this little bird really calling me to task? I would like to think so, but can I be sure?

The word *transcendence* comes from Latin *trans* (meaning "across" or "over") and *scandere* ("to climb"). A precise image is embedded in this word's etymology. The image refers to physical experiences, like climbing over walls or clambering across fences. Transcendence means a boundary is breached, an abyss overcome.

Experiences of transcendence ignore the psychic walls created artificially by human consciousness and its conditioning. They expose another reality. Material reality and spiritual reality – the visible world of bodies and tangible objects and the invisible world of the unconscious, the psyche, the soul, the beyond – belong to a single, undivided whole. This is the picture offered, a unified field that Jung called the objective psyche.

Walls exist and need to be climbed over because human consciousness inevitably creates them. These walls are artifacts of a necessarily limited point of view. And their reality is convincing most of the time. Doubt speaks: Does transcendence reveal something true, or does it create seductive deceptions? What is the ontological status of such altered states of awareness? How you answer this question will say a great deal about your basic assumptions and philosophical commitments.

Let me describe a series of experiences of transcendence that happened to me personally. I invite you to reflect on them with me. They do not offer incontestable proof of the soul's transcendence, and they will not settle all doubts and disputes, but they have pushed me to question some of my own deepest assumptions about the impenetrability of the walls that our modern ego-consciousness has constructed.

Several years ago an aged friend of mine died. I had known her for more than ten years, and in the course of all that time we had had many profound conversations. Irene was Catholic and a vowed religious and believed without reservation in the reality of God and the afterlife. I am a Protestant rationalist and have a stubborn habit of conscious doubt. I was a skeptic about such matters, but I did not question the sincerity of her beliefs and never challenged her certainties. I would simply listen respectfully when we entered that territory.

Irene became disabled in later life and was confined to a wheelchair. She enjoyed telling me that when she died and went to heaven the first thing she wanted to do there was to dance. She loved to imagine her body whole again and capable of full movement. This is what she looked forward to most of all, even more than to meeting loved ones and the religiously famous. In her youth she had loved to dance, and she grieved the loss of her physical mobility and independence.

Shortly before her death, I read in a newspaper that Pope John Paul II had confirmed the sainthood of Edith Stein and would canonize her in Rome at St. Peter's. Irene had connections in Rome, so I asked her if she thought it would be possible for me to obtain tickets for the canonization. She made a phone call and assured me that when the time came, I would have seats. I thanked her profusely.

After Irene received a diagnosis of terminal pancreatic cancer, she died quickly, asking her doctors to withhold unrealistic treatment. She was prepared to leave her body. I was disappointed in the timing of her death because I was just then finishing a book on transformation and had wanted to share this with her. I knew she would have enjoyed reading it, and we could have had some further conversations about this theme.

My wife and I did have the privilege of being with her for an hour on the day before she passed away. She was in and out of consciousness and barely showed awareness of our presence, but I am quite sure she could observe us from another place in her psyche. We kissed her farewell, wishing her a good journey into the valley of the shadow of death. I knew she was as well prepared for this final experience of life as anyone can be.

On the day of her funeral, we were surprised to learn that the site of her service had been changed to a larger church. We had come to the wrong place and at the wrong time. The service was to be held several hours later in another part of town. Our car had been parked in a lovely garden behind the home, and as we drove away I asked my wife to check the back seat. Something had gotten in and was flapping around in the rear window. It was an extremely hot day in Chicago, and the windows and doors had been closed tight because the car had air conditioning.

She turned to the rear window and exclaimed in surprise, "It's a butterfly!"

"Impossible," I said. "How could a butterfly have gotten into our car all locked up?"

But sure enough, it was a large brown butterfly with bits of blue on its wings. And it was determined to stay in the rear window of our car for the whole trip. I opened all the windows, offering it an escape and hoping it would fly away, but it refused to leave. Even after the funeral service, the butterfly continued to accompany us as we drove homeward. We began to speak of it jokingly as Irene.

"Well, okay, Irene has decided to come home with us!"

When we got home, it was dark. My wife reached her hand into the back of the car in hopes that the butterfly would now accept the invitation to make an exit. Previously this had not worked, but this time the butterfly hopped onto her hand and sat tight. We called our friend Joyce from inside the house to come out and see. She had also known Irene quite well.

As we stood outside together under a streetlight, Irene the butterfly jumped to the ground and began an amazing dance at our feet. Around and around she went in a frenzy of motion. Suddenly I remembered Irene's ardent hope to dance again in eternity, and I burst out, "Well, Irene I see you've made it! You're dancing!"

At this moment, I was no longer a Protestant rationalist and my agnosticism vanished completely. The boundaries between this world and the next had been breached. I could only believe that in this moment we were living both in time and eternity. Surely this was Irene dancing in the form of a butterfly.

The butterfly flew off, and we knew we had witnessed something extraordinary.

The next morning, our friend Joyce telephoned. She said, "Do you know what happened to the butterfly?"

"No."

"It came home with me in my car! And then it flew off in the direction of Dorothy's garden." Dorothy had been one of Irene's lifelong best friends.

About a year passed when, thanks to Irene's earlier intervention, I was able to get tickets for Edith Stein's canonization in Rome.

The canonization ceremony took place in St. Peter's Square on October 11, 1998. I had been interested in the case of Edith Stein for some years. She was a Jewish convert to Roman Catholicism who became a Carmelite nun in the 1930s and died a Jewish-Christian martyr in Auschwitz in 1942. She was also a distinguished philosopher and had been the favorite pupil of Edmund Husserl. I was interested in her case for many reasons and had read some of her works and several biographies of her life. In addition, I had never seen a canonization service before. So I was in a state of heightened anticipation as my wife and I and a couple of friends made our way to the choice seats reserved for us, thanks to the help of Irene and her friends in Rome.

The service itself was deeply moving. This elderly pope, so humbled by age and physical decline, who could barely move forward out of St. Peter's to his chair on the platform under his own power, presided for three hours over a service that was very special for him, too. Both he and Edith Stein were born and grew up in Poland, and he has been intensely involved in healing the historical conflict between Christians and Jews. The ritual, the music, the crowd of seventy thousand people from all parts of the world, the illustrious cardinals and politicians on the platform with the pope – Helmut Kohl was there – all of this contributed to the impressive effect. The invisible world became quite palpable in that atmosphere, understandably so. But nothing could have prepared me for what happened as the service was drawing to a close.

As we were standing for the final prayer of benediction, the pope began intoning his blessing in Latin. The text of this prayer was presented in four languages, and I was following the pope's unclear diction as best I could understand it. When he arrived at the line, "Ex hoc nunc et usque in saeculum" ("Von nun an bis in Ewigkeit," "Ora e sempre," "Now and forever"), an astonishing thing happened. A brown butterfly with blue bits of color on its wings appeared out of nowhere from that crowd of thousands and alighted on the open page. It perched quietly on the words *Ora e sempre* and stayed there.

At first I could not take in what was happening. It was a total surprise. I had seen no butterflies in that sea of human faces before this. I was stunned. Where had this butterfly come from? We were in the middle of a huge crowd in a giant city, not in a garden. I looked around in astonishment and could hardly believe my eyes. There were no other butterflies to be seen.

My wife gasped, too. "It's the same butterfly!" she whispered.

Sure enough, the colors were the same as the one in Chicago. (Our friends beside us did not know the story of Irene the butterfly, but they were nonetheless also surprised to see a butterfly in this unlikely place and sitting on my prayerbook.)

Is this Irene? I wondered to myself in amazement.

The butterfly took to the air as the pope said "Amen" and disappeared in the direction of the altar some one hundred meters in front of us. My fantasy was that it joined the other spirits and angels so palpably present in St. Peter's Square that bright day in October.

This experience and others like it have led me to reflect more deeply than before on the reality of the soul and also on the nature of symbols.

It is common to say that the butterfly is a well-known symbol for the immortal soul. In classical antiquity, it was widely believed that the soul left the body in the form of a butterfly at the moment of death. The psyche is often represented as a butterfly in paintings and written texts. In Christian thought, the body has sometimes been conceived of as the caterpillar stage of life and death as a metamorphosis into another and more splendid stage of the soul's existence, the butterfly stage. This belief is not confined to Mediterranean cultures. The Aztecs believed the butterfly symbolized the soul and was exhaled by the dying. "A butterfly fluttering among the flowers represented the soul of the warrior who had fallen on the battlefield" (DS). I knew well this metaphor for the soul.

To say that this butterfly represented Irene's soul might not be just a metaphorical expression, however. Perhaps it was true in a stronger and more ontological sense. Was not this butterfly – a real, tangible, physical butterfly with its own life history in the world of time and space – more than a metaphor? Was it perhaps a symbol? And if so, what is a symbol, really? Do symbols tell us something about reality that we do not already know?

Symbols are not signs, as Jung repeated many times. A sign is a humanly designed image or object that stands intentionally for something else. Signs are made and used by humans for specific purposes. A sign must represent a known meaning, otherwise it is worthless. The black marks on this paper that spell out the word *butterfly* are a sign for the insect that flits through the garden in summer. This sign directs the mind's attention to something else that is known. If I know how to read a language, the signs on the page make sense to me. A sign must begin and end within the realm of what is known. There can be no mystery here or the result is confusion. Symbols, by contrast, present the unknown; they do not re-present the known. If we said that the butterfly was a sign for Irene's soul, we would have to be able to say that we know exactly what her soul is and that the butterfly was consciously intended by someone to represent her soul. Medieval people did believe God used nature in this way, but no longer do most people think this way. We are not so certain about God.

(Metaphors are not the same as symbols either. Metaphors are mental comparisons. "I'm goin' fishing" can be a metaphorical expression that says, "I'm going to relax, not worry, leave work behind." Metaphors often create shortcuts and condense a whole network of meanings into an image or an expression of a few words. They are necessary and convenient and often highly ingenious ways of thinking and expressing one's thoughts and feelings. Metaphors are not signs in that they do not point to something else. They communicate meanings and intentions and often open up new avenues for thought and reflection. They are the product of creative imagination. Symbols are more like signs than they are like metaphors. Unlike metaphors, they are not products of creative imagination and they are not mental in nature.)

Like signs, symbols are objects that point to something else, but what they point to is unknown and unknowable. They capture a mystery and leave us stunned with an altered sense of reality. They seem to go beyond our knowing and unite the visible and invisible. They convince us of the reality of the soul beyond what is known or can be known by conscious means and rational explication.

Not all butterflies are symbols. Some are simply insects. It is important to know the difference. One cannot say simply that butterflies are symbols for the soul. That would turn them into signs. Sometimes a butterfly is a symbol, sometimes it is not. The same butterfly can be a symbol one time and just an insect another.

In Irene's case, the butterfly was an insect, literally, but it was also a soul, symbolically. The insect brought with it another presence. In this doubling, the physical object, a butterfly, became a synthesis of matter and spirit, a uniting object. This "double object," which defines the term *symbol,* is both material and spiritual. There is no division. You cannot say that the butterfly is an insect that stands for a soul (a sign), because in that moment it is the soul (as well as an insect). In this moment, we are privileged to see reality as the unconscious sees it, following Jung's observation that the unconscious does not observe a difference between matter and spirit. They are identical.

The word *symbol* is taken from the Greek *symbolon. Symbola* are two pieces of a coin that the contracting parties have broken between them; each keeps one part. *Symballo,* the verb, means "to bring together, to unite." When the two pieces of coin are brought together again by the contracting parties, wholeness is restored and identity affirmed.

A symbol, then, brings together two separated pieces of an original whole, matter and spirit. This united whole portrays the reality of the soul. And this is what Irene the butterfly teaches.

To look to religion for a moment, Roman Catholic understanding of the Mass is that it is a symbol. In the literal material of bread and wine, the spiritual Christ is present. In the ritual of the Mass, spirit and matter are re-united in the symbol. The Protestant Reformers, on the other hand, understood the communion service as a sign. It is a memorial to Jesus, who died for our sins so many long years ago. The service stands for something important that happened in the past. It does not re-create it in the present.

So is a symbol, then, not just the product of human interpretation? Catholics interpret communion one way, Protestants another. So what? With my eyes, I saw a butterfly, and I interpreted this sensate impression as Irene. But I have seen many butterflies before and after and rarely have they struck me as anything but butterflies. Mostly butterflies are just lepidoptera. Perhaps I have thought once or twice, on looking out over a summer meadow, "Well, isn't it interesting that these may be the souls of Aztec warriors flitting about this field of flaxen blossoms?" But that was strictly a deliberate mental act of interpretation. Interpretation is based on conscious knowledge. Dream interpretation, for instance, may simply translate the signs of dream life into the known theories of psychoanalysts.

When I saw that butterfly dancing at my feet under the streetlight, however, I did not make an interpretation by using my conscious knowledge and theories. I exclaimed spontaneously and automatically, "Dance, Irene, dance!" Irene was there. This was not dependent on my knowledge that butterflies have traditionally counted as images representing the soul. I would have said and felt the same thing had I been an illiterate who never heard of such a myth. Irene's presence was as plain in this dancing butterfly as was my wife's presence in the form of her body. Irene's soul had simply taken another form. To me, this was self-evident.

Yet skepticism remains. This could have been mere coincidence, a coincidence that Irene's funeral coincided with the butterfly in my car. And another coincidence that she had spoken of dancing in the afterlife and now this butterfly was dancing at my feet. And still another that a butterfly happened to alight on the words "now and forever" at

Edith Stein's canonization service, at which, also coincidentally, my attendance had been arranged by Irene. Coincidences happen. Let's be realistic. Still, this is a lot of coincidences happening all around a single theme.

The strong feeling of meaningful coincidence, which evokes a profound shudder of awe, elicits an involuntary capitulation of intellectual reserve, and brings the walls of separation down, is what Jung called synchronicity. In the experience of transcendence and of the symbolic, timing is all-important. It is uncanny timeliness that creates a context for what the Greeks called *kairos,* a kind of time in which the individual moment is like no other. It is packed with meaning and associations, and objects are doubled and also become invisible presences. The sense data written on our retinas tell us about more than the sensate world. It is a moment of annunciation, of revelation. It is then that we see the whole fabric of reality spread out before us, and matter and spirit are not apart but single and one.

A symbol, as opposed to a sign or a metaphor or a simile or a mere image, brings the opening to transcendence with it. One does not "read" symbols or "interpret" them. One experiences them. They are numinous. The symbol breaches the barrier between matter and spirit, conscious and unconscious, time and eternity. It reveals fundamental wholeness.

If this is indeed the nature of the symbol, what does it mean for the practice of psychotherapy, especially for those who claim to work with symbols and with the symbolic nature of dreams and other unconsciously based phenomena? This question should make us a little uncomfortable. Have we really thought this through? Most therapists have not.

The first and strongest note to sound, I feel, is the importance of respect for the reality of the soul. As psychotherapists, we must take up matters of the psyche with the utmost respect, especially if we are handling symbols. To cite Jung: "whatever explanation or interpretation does to it [i.e., the symbol], we do to our own souls as well, with corresponding results for our own well-being" (1951, par. 271). We must recognize that in dealing with symbols we are handling objects that imply transcendence and affect us both materially and spiritually.

Let me give an example of a symbol's emergence in praxis. A woman who had been through surgery for breast cancer a little more than five years before this session, reported the following dream:

> *I find myself on Golden Gate Bridge in San Francisco, and suddenly I realize that I am falling off the bridge into the bay far below. I drop into the water and seem to be okay. But then I see a great white fish coming toward me. It looks like a shark. I am terrified that it is going to attack me. Suddenly there is a telepathic connection between us, however, and the fish assures me that it means no harm. In fact, the fish "tells" me that it is going to help me. It says that on its back there is a space carved out especially for me, exactly fitted to my size, where I can lie down calmly and place my arms into a comfortable position for the ride. The fish will carry me to safety. I awake greatly comforted and relieved.*

The patient had few specific associations to this dream. Of course, she knew of the Golden Gate Bridge and had seen pictures and movies about sharks and great white fish. Her fear of attack she associated to her worries about a return of cancer. At the moment, the doctors had recently told her, she was healthy. But she was medically trained and knew that risks remained. Associating to the dream and its life-threatening features, she continued reflecting on her concerns about health and her fear of death.

In American mythology, of course, the Golden Gate Bridge and the great white fish occupy special positions. They are cultural icons. The Golden Gate Bridge lies at the far western edge of the American continent, the furthest point on what was once the Great Frontier. It stands in a place of supreme liminality, at the boundary between the inhabited continent and the vast unknown waters of the largest ocean on earth. The Golden Gate Bridge is fixed on the threshold of the collective unconscious. As it turns out, this bridge, so aptly named "Golden Gate," is also associated with death. Many suicides take place here. It is a famous jumping-off place into the great unknown.

The great white fish is the main character of the classic American novel, *Moby Dick*, by Herman Melville. In the novel, the white whale is an image of God – an ambiguous, awesome, overwhelming force that cannot be overcome or destroyed by human will. In religious iconography, too, the fish is an image of God. Christ is often represented as a great fish, the souls of his followers as lesser fish.

This dream made a deep impression on the patient. Discussing the images of the dream in therapy, and the associations both personal and collective, added substance to its monumental stature. The patient realized that it was symbolic dream, one that brings together the material and spiritual worlds. The great white fish of the dream was not only a mental image, a sign or a metaphor. It possessed independent ontological standing.

When a symbol becomes manifest in a dream, it occupies a privileged ontological position. It is a double object, both a mental image and a spiritual reality. This duality is captured in the English word *psychic*. If something is "psychic," it bridges between the world of mental imagery and the world of nonmental objects. The psyche itself bridges the boundary between inner and outer worlds, between that which is strictly speaking only subjective and that which is objective and exists beyond the individual's mental world of thoughts, feelings, and perceptions. Jung used the sometimes puzzling term *objective psyche* to refer to this fact.

The patient carried this dream actively and resolutely in her consciousness for the rest of her life, which turned out to be only two more years. Shortly after having the dream, she felt a lump under her skin, underwent tests, and was given the bad news that the cancer had metastasized and was now to be found in her lungs and other parts of her body. She began to make final arrangements regarding her earthly affairs.

What difference does it make to regard the great white fish in the dream as a symbol? First of all, it brings into play a strong note of respect for this image. We must respect a dream symbol that unites visible and invisible worlds and knits together the fabric torn between matter and spirit. The dream conveys transcendence.

This realization about the nature of symbols makes an essential difference in psychotherapy. For instance, if we said that the fish image represented the patient's fear of death and that her defenses then converted it into a figure of consolation, or simply that it represents her death wish, we remain strictly within the limited field of subjectivity and interpretations based on psychological theory. Here we leave the dream phenomena behind in favor of a pet idea. Theory may teach that we have a death wish, for instance, and so we can suppose that the fish, which represents the threat of death in the waters of the unconscious, offers a wish fulfillment. Or we might say that from Sunday school, the patient (who was indeed a lapsed Catholic) knew that Christ is represented as a fish and that her dream is conveying this image to compensate for her fear of death in the dark waters of the unconscious. She is threatened with extinction, and the dream comforts her – another interpretation based on theory. Or we could interpret the white fish as representing her mother, who was both threatening and comforting for the dreamer in her childhood. The patient did have a highly ambivalent relation to her mother. But again, this leaves the dream within the realm of personal complexes and memory residues and does not take into account the symbolic aspect of the dream.

If the fish is a symbol, on the other hand, what then? It has a different ontological status. It breathes reality in a wholly different way. It speaks of a comforter that is real, from "out there," from beyond the boundaries of subjectivity altogether, from beyond the territory of all that is known or learned or captured in our conscious knowledge bases. The fish is a god who speaks telepathically, who has prepared an individual place in its body for the patient, who offers to carry the patient to safety. The dream becomes a revelation.

This same fish reappeared in a number of other dreams as the patient went through the last stages of her life and suffered the agonies of radiation therapy, chemotherapy, and all the other remedies known to medicine. She was not to be cured of her disease. And yet the fish remained a presence in her consciousness. It became her dear companion in the darkest moments of despair and fear. The transcendence it offered became the "ground of being" for her. She returned, too, to her religious faith, to prayer, to trust that her soul would leave the body upon her death and come to rest in an individual place especially prepared for her. The dream had shown her that there is an individualized place for her in the fish's body, exactly fitted to her requirements. The soul is individual and it stays intact. She died a horrible death physically, but she was at peace psychologically.

Once a dream image is recognized as symbolic, it retains its power to unite matter and spirit, visible and invisible, conscious and unconscious. It maintains its transcendence.

I attended this patient's funeral recently. She was eulogized by the priest and honored by her many friends and her family. And for the final musical selection of the service, she had chosen the gospel hymn, "Swing low, sweet chariot." Its words capture the feeling of hard-won faith and trust:

> *I looked over Jordan and what did I see,*
> *Coming for to carry me home?*
> *A band of angels coming after me,*
> *Coming for to carry me home.*

She had seen them coming in her dream of the great white fish. She has now been carried home.

Not all butterflies are souls, nor are all dream images symbols. Most dreams simply compensate in a daily fashion for the one-sidedness of conscious attitudes. Much of psychotherapy is conducted on the level of everyday consciousness. Problems are presented, solutions are sought, psychodynamic interpretations are made and can be useful.

Symbols do emerge in therapy, however. They do so as they do in life generally – with surprising and meaningful timeliness, in moments of *kairos*, synchronistically. And they lead to the experience of transcendence. When this happens, there is an opportunity to see things from the viewpoint of the unconscious, where matter and spirit are simply two aspects of one reality.

Two weeks after my patient's funeral, her daughter called me. She wanted to share a story. Her lifelong pen pal in Sweden had just telephoned to say that she had recently received her brief note telling of her mother's death. She was sitting in the garden when she opened her mail, and as she reading this sad and surprising news a large colorful butterfly suddenly perched on top of the small card. She was astonished. How could it have chosen a space so tiny to land on? From there it flitted to her arm where it remained for several minutes. Suddenly, she said, it became clear who this was. "It was your mother, I'm sure of it," she cried out over the telephone. "So colorful, so beautiful – just like your mother. And so alive!"

References

Jung, C. G. 1951. The psychology of the child archetype. *Collected Works,* vol. 9i. Princeton, N.J.: Princeton University Press, 1959, 1968.

Dreams – Hidden Treasures of the Unconscious

※

Margaret Zulaski, OSF

There is a secret energy driving things.

—Rumi

Introduction

IRENE DUGAN AS A SPIRITUAL DIRECTOR, A MENTOR, AND A FRIEND manifested the incarnation of the Divine in a unique human being. She was attuned to symbolic language, and she evoked a trust of image and imagination. She had keen insight for comprehending the movement of spirit in both the inner life and outer circumstances of a person. Because Irene viewed spiritual experience not simply as a private matter, her way of being with you challenged and demanded incarnation. She believed that spiritual experience calls for a response that incarnates the experience of the Divine via our way of being in relationship to others and to the concerns of the world. Her mentoring invited recognition of hidden potential and the possibilities of individual talents and also helped shed light on how we diminish our expression and participation in life. She was both able to receive the uniqueness of the person and willing to demand the wholeness of a person.

Psyche and Soul in Human Personality

In the last century we have come a long way in understanding human experience as being both psychological and spiritual. From dichotomous approaches that polarized psychology and spirituality into opposing camps, we have turned to views in which psychology and spirituality share common ground. Carl Gustav Jung's depth psychology contributed greatly to this paradigm shift toward an integrative understanding of the psyche and soul of human experience. In Jung's view, the psyche includes the totality of both consciousness and the unconscious, while soul is understood as the human capacity to connect with creative and universal patterns.

Jung recognized the necessity of a relational exchange between ego consciousness, defined as the "I" that is known, and the unconscious, defined most simply as the unknown. He considered questions that are familiar to one who seeks religious meaning: Who am I in relation to the unknown? How do I encounter the unknown? How does the unknown affect my life? He emphasized the use of dreams as a fundamental means for establishing the relationship of ego to the unconscious.

Jung's term *individuation* refers to the process of becoming a more conscious and more distinct individual as a result of developing a receptivity to the unconscious dimension of one's personality. Individuation is an ongoing process of becoming who we are meant to be; this identifies a potential wholeness of personality (Samuels 1986, p. 76). Individuation is a way of working things out as we go along, a way of discovering a sense of meaning and value in everyday life.

I find Jung's depth psychology compatible with an incarnational spirituality that views the religious journey as a process of individual transformation directed by the movement of "God within" the human person. Both individuation and the incarnational spiritual journey emphasize an ongoing process, a way of becoming attuned to the unknown or to the mystery of the God in the person. For both, wholeness or holiness is not a goal to be achieved; it is the ongoing search for meaning that matters. Both accept that life involves paradox and mystery.

Jung's experience and lifetime of scholarship led him to propose the concept of the Self as an archetype of wholeness, that is, an intelligent center of the psyche. He described the Self as purposeful because it functions as an innate urge for our wholeness. As a mover and shaper for wholeness, the Self is an inner guide that attempts to break through to ego consciousness. When attention is given to dreams, the symbolic communication from the Self in dream images can lead to recognizing what is necessary for the path to wholeness.

Jung's concept of the "Self" asserts a religious function in the human psyche, much as incarnational spirituality affirms "God within" as the source of transformation for wholeness. This similarity is evident when Jung writes of the Self as the center:

> I have called this centre the Self. Intellectually the Self is no more than a psychological concept, a construct that serves to express an unknowable essence which we cannot grasp as such, since by definition it transcends our powers of comprehension. It might equally be called "God within us." (1928, par. 399)

This is not to say "Self is God," because the mystery of God is beyond knowing, and words cannot grasp this mystery. Rather, the words *Self* and *God within* convey that which can never be fully known. The Self (God within) directs energy from the depths that can arouse our attention and disturb the status quo; that energy has a purpose—movement for the journey into wholeness.

Dreams as Thresholds to Inner Realms

In order to discuss a Jungian approach to dreams, it is necessary to clarify the terms *ego consciousness* and the *unconscious*. Ego, as the center of consciousness, directs the focus of concentration, makes choices, remembers, and reflects on experience. Ego consciousness refers to our familiar sense of self, the "I" that says, "This is me." Ego consciousness is characterized by habitual ways of thinking and behaving, a tendency for maintaining a sense of security based on what is known. We are more likely to recognize the ego's fixed point of view in others than in ourselves, when we notice another person's position as close minded or inflexible. Ego has a particular selectivity as "I" holds on to some facts and dismisses others. Ego denies certain information in order to preserve an established self-image. The reality of "denial," an inability to see the consequences of one's behavior, is well known in addictive behavior.

We can get an outer view of ourselves by looking in a mirror, by recognizing our personal history, and by noticing the responses of others to our behavior. The dream provides an inner view, a mirror of our inner self. Dreams often reveal, in images, information that the ego is lacking. The perspective of ego may be compared to the area lit up by the beam of a flashlight; it is a limited viewpoint. All that is in the dark area beyond the flashlight beam is more or less unconscious. Some areas of the unconscious are retrievable, such as memories of the past, which are not always in the flashlight beam of the ego. But there are vast areas of the unconscious that are simply unknown to the limited view of ego consciousness. Dreams actively reveal an inner reality through images that present something unknown that seeks attention. According to Jung, when ego consciousness develops receptivity to images from the unconscious via dreams, there is a greater possibility of coming to a wholeness of our own personality, that is, becoming the person we are meant to be (1934, par. 352).

A contemporary Jungian analyst, Peter Mudd, characterizes the "core dynamic" of the unconscious in relationship to ego consciousness as

> animating, enlivening, inspiring, or fascinating the ego by presenting it with what it needs in the next step toward selfhood. Often in numinous symbolic costume, it carries those balancing, completing elements of personality that have been eliminated in service of building an identity, or which have never been conscious but are now needed for adaptation. These symbolic elements are the new forms of being that change our lives, our identities, our behavior, and our world. (1998, p. 10)

Attending to dreams is a method for drawing upon the hidden treasures of the unconscious. By exploring dream images we participate in the creative unfolding of our own true personality. We learn different perspectives regarding situations in life. We learn that we are more than ego, and that there is direction available from within, from the Self.

Beginnings

I began paying attention to my dreams twenty-some years ago because a repetitive dream disturbed me. In the dream, I am driving a car in the dark of night on a country road when suddenly several boys, as young as three-year-olds, run across on the road in front of me. I am terrified that I might not be able to stop the car and that I might kill a child.

That fear jolted me from my sleep. After ignoring the first couple of dreams like this, the dream occurred with some alteration – the boys were not only darting across the road but they stopped to face me, daring me to stop or hit them. At that time, I was unfamiliar with the symbolic nature of dreams, and I feared I would actually have a car accident and kill a child. That thought disturbed me and led me to speak with someone who was familiar with the language of dreams.

At the time of these dreams, I had taken on a difficult job. I lacked a sense of direction in my new position, and I felt tension about how to perform this job. Would I follow what others had done before me or would I find my own way to go about it? What did the unconscious give me in this dream? Driving along a road was an image of going the usual route, the way of ego, while the boys provided an image of something new that required my attention. In the dream, from the driver's point of view, I was terrified of being reckless, while from the point of view of the boys there is a reckless abandon in their play. I found that the image of the boys playing in the road revealed an adventurous and daring energy that I could bring to my consideration of how to proceed with my new position. Could I risk a more creative approach to this job? Would my employer accept my plan? The dream showed that rambunctious "boy" energy was available for my work, but I (ego) had to find how to incarnate that, how to apply this energy to my situation in life.

Dreams come to us from the unconscious in symbolic language that is not easily grasped by the logical, rational mind of ego consciousness. In a 1933 lecture, Jung suggested,

> One would do well to treat every dream as though it were a totally unknown object. Look at it from all sides, take it in your hand, carry it about with you, let your imagination play around with it. (par. 320)

Dream images present us with the unexpected (suddenly everything changes), with the unusual (animals speak), with the paradoxical (what is dead becomes alive again). If we can hold back from following the familiar and obvious meaning of a dream image, then we can explore the image until something captures our attention and leads to new meaning.

Sometimes a dream image intensely affects us. Whether the intensity is nightmarish or awesome, it is certainly gripping and not easily forgotten. Such images are called numinous because of their compelling power—the image refuses to fade; the image haunts us and demands our reflective consideration. Like my dream of the boys, some dream images keep coming up. These examples of dream images with a numinous quality show how the meaning of the image is unique to the dreamer.

A religious woman in Chicago dreams:

> They are building a chapel in the attic of the retreat house. Irene Dugan
> is in charge. Irene and a male priest are arranging the altar. The place is
> beautiful beyond imagination. The room is filled with a golden glow. A
> map of the world is on the wall. At first the lines on the map do not con-
> nect. Then the lines that begin in Chicago go out to all parts of the world.
> Suddenly the lines light up and they are all connected. Deep emotion fills
> me when I see this happen.

Because of its awesome and beautiful quality, this dream deeply affected the dreamer and brought with it feelings of hope and love. In the dream, she felt an atmosphere of golden light that totally carried her away to a sense of the Divine. This dream delivered to the dreamer what words cannot convey, something about the Divine connection in all things.

A young man living with AIDS dreams:

> I am in a room that is like a small and dingy apartment. I open a door
> and see that there is a narrow crawl space that leads like a tunnel to a
> large open space. I see at the end of the crawl space a view that opens to a
> large garden filled with brilliant colored flowers. I try to get into the crawl
> space but it feels too small.

At the time of this dream, this young man was feeling ill. He recognized how he felt constricted by his illness. The view of the beautiful garden expressed his desire for more life at a time when he was feeling particularly low. This dream impressed him with a sense of his own resistance to getting on with his life. He recognized that because of his AIDS diagnosis he had been expecting death and mourning the loss of his unlived life. The garden impressed him with a desire for life.

A middle-aged woman dreams:

> *I am lying down resting in an outdoor place. Suddenly, a large python approaches my feet. I am terrified as the snake moves over me. Then it coils itself up, resting at my side. I awake frozen in fear, feeling like this could kill me.*

This vivid and terrifying image left this woman feeling a sense of dread and repulsion. But she also noticed the strangeness of the combination of images: the snake as life threatening and the snake at rest. She thought about situations in her life that felt like death but also brought about new life. The numinous snake image led her to reflect on the elemental power of the snake and on her own relationship to power.

A numinous image can stay with us for many years; it is a gift that carries with it energy with potential for transformation (Stein 1998, p. 41). The dream image pulls ego consciousness in the direction of the unconscious in order to reveal something unknown yet quite particular to one's situation in life. Dreams reveal something new to our awareness; they may reveal a conflict that requires attention, or they provide direction on the path of wholeness, or both!

A middle-aged woman executive received this dream image: "I leave my office and find the corridors crowded with cows. They seem to be everywhere and no one takes notice of them but me." After reflecting on this curious image of cows in the corporate world, the idea of sacred cows popped into her mind and seemed to have meaning for her. She wondered what are the sacred cows of this corporation, and she wondered how she would have to meet up with them. Catching on to the dream requires the development of an attitude of attention to symbolic images followed by a choice to value the symbolic image and then find some way to express the meaning of it in actual life situations.

The most important practice in dream work is developing a receptive attitude toward the unknown. Developing an openness to dreams is a way of cultivating soul, because one engages with symbols that connect with the Self, energy within that directs the movement toward wholeness. The necessary opening for this connection is the ego's initiative, that is, a decision is made to receive the symbolic language of dreams as meaningful. This receptive attitude requires willingness to admit that the viewpoint of the ego is limited and also willingness to set aside preconceived ideas about ourselves in order to seek direction from within. By attending to images from dreams, we develop a relationship to the unconscious so that the wisdom of the Self can guide and affect our life.

Practical Approaches

Be prepared to record dreams by having pen and paper ready. A dream can fade within minutes of awakening from sleep. Write whatever memory of the dream you can capture just to get started. Write the dream in as much detail as possible, including the emotions and sensations of the dream. Telling the dream to someone is another way of accepting the value of the dream.

Consider the dream as a fact, as something meaningful. Recalling the dream, what particular image stands out? What evokes attention? An image may stand out in a dream because it is so unusual, such as "guests arriving at a dinner party and there is a skunk in the midst of them." Often a dream follows a dramatic sequence that conveys a problematic situation with particular characters in a particular setting. It is common that a dream narrative culminates in a sudden change. For example, "I am leaving my house when suddenly the steps are gone and there is a deep drop-off from the doorway to the ground." Such sudden changes in a dream clearly beckon for attention.

It is best to begin the dream reflection by considering your current circumstances. Does anything experienced in the past few days show any similarity to the dream image? For example, in the "house without steps" image, the dreamer wonders "Was anything recently like a sudden drop-off or like a disconnection from the ground?" Focus on your present situation and ask yourself, "How is this dream related to my life?" The dream may simply suggest another perspective on things or it may offer support or encouragement. The dream may also confront the dreamer with something that requires more attention, such as an unresolved relational problem or a past trauma.

Linking dream images to personal memories is another way to make meaningful connections. For example, a character in a dream may remind the dreamer of someone from her/his past. The dream may also have a setting from the past. Consider how these particular characters and memories parallel current situations in life or how they call attention to something that may require active expression.

If consulting a dictionary for help in understanding dreams, do not look for a definitive meaning of a dream image. A symbol dictionary of any substance provides multiple interpretations for any given image and includes information from many cultures. When considering the interpretation of a dream image, stay close to the felt sense of what the image means. Where does this image take you, the dreamer, in knowing yourself or in expressing yourself? What new information does the dream image offer?

Play with the dream images. If there is an animal in the dream, observe that animal and look for what the nature of that animal communicates. Elaborate the dream image by allowing any related images to come up for consideration. Find parallel motifs from film, myth, or fairy tales. Some images lend themselves to elaboration through creative expressions such as drawing, sculpting, or dance. Recall the dream of the young man who could see the beautiful garden but could not reach it. There are parallel images in the story of *The Secret Garden* by Frances Hodgson Burnett, in which a boy believes that he is crippled when he actually is constricted by fear. This dreamer could further elaborate the dream by physical movement, like moving through the constriction in the tunnel, by drawing a picture of the garden with all its richness of color, or simply by bringing beautiful flowers into his home.

Dream work is Jung's method for developing a connection for an ongoing relationship of ego with the unconscious. The connection results from an interaction of ego's receptivity to the dream and of the activity generated by the Self that propels images and symbols toward the consciousness of the dreamer. It is not always easy to catch on to dream symbols. The work requires patience. Attend and stay with the images until their meaning is gradually revealed. That the dream image influences the dreamer matters more than that the dreamer comes up with an explanation of the dream. The symbolic language of dreams is mysterious and cannot be completely understood; it is like a Zen koan or a gospel parable that actively shifts our familiar perceptions of reality.

Catching on to the symbolic communication of dreams means that the symbol has an effect, the symbol moves the dreamer. A symbol carries energy that directs us to a creative response in our life situation and suggests trying something new or considering something different than our usual patterns. We get motivation, we get a change of attitude, or we get a change of behavior. Such transformation in the religious language of incarnational spirituality is the breakthrough of the Divine in human experience, in ordinary events, and in relationships.

In the example of the woman whose dream showed her cows in the corporation, her interpretation of the need to address the sacred cows of that organization had meaning for her. If she carries through with behavior that does confront the sacred cows, she is participating in the transformation of that corporation. Furthermore, if she remains open to seeing the sacred in the business of the corporation, then her incarnation of the sacred may, like yeast in dough, affect the whole organization. This shows that reflection on one's dreams can go beyond the individual to affect the human community.

The life of Francis of Assisi gives another example of what happens when a symbol breaks through to ego consciousness. While at prayer, in a dreamlike state, Francis heard the image of the crucified Christ speak to him, "Rebuild my church." At first, he attempted to incarnate the meaning of this literally by doing construction work to restore dilapidated churches. He did not immediately realize how living his life with integrity created a new way of being religious. His experience would become the foundation for an entire new movement in the life of the church. Francis of Assisi also wrote a new, inspired rule of life for the religious community he founded. Acquiring the papal approval necessary for the formal foundation of a new religious order was no easy task.

It is remarkable to note that Pope Innocent III had a dream at the same time that Francis traveled to Rome to seek approval of his rule of life. In the dream, the pope saw "the church of Saint John Lateran threatening to collapse, and a religious of small and shabby appearance, supporting it on his shoulders" (Armstrong 2000, p. 97). Upon meeting Francis, the pope recognized the image of the small and shabby man from the dream; he accepted Francis and confirmed his proposed rule of life. Francis thought that his life project was small, but it was the way he lived his life, an individuation process of becoming who he was meant to be, that is what rebuilt the church of his time.

Attention to dreams is a way an individual may connect with the Self (God within) and receive direction for living one's own integrity. Those who have gone before us and who lived the journey of wholeness demonstrate how consciously working on one's own life is significant to the whole human community.

Grateful acknowledgment to Peter Mudd for his generosity as teacher and as consultant for this paper.

References

Armstrong, R., J. Hellman, and W. Short. 2000. *Francis of Assisi: The Founder*. New York: New City Press.

Jung, C. G. 1928. The relations between the ego and the unconscious. In *Collected Works*, vol. 7:227–241. Princeton, N.J.: Princeton University Press, 1966.

_____. 1933. The meaning of psychology for modern man. In *Collected Works*, vol. 10:134–156. Princeton, N.J.: Princeton University Press, 1970.

_____. 1934. The practical use of dreams anlysis. In *Collected Works*, vol. 16:139–161. Princeton, N.J.: Princeton University Press, 1966.

Mudd, P. 1998. Jung and the split feminine. Part 2. *The Round Table Review* 6/1:1–10.

Samuels, A., B. Shorter, and F. Plaut. 1986. *A Critical Dictionary of Jungian Analysis*. New York: Routledge and Kegan Paul.

Stein, M. 1998. *Transformation: Emergence of the Self*. College Station, Texas: Texas A&M University Press.

Loving Life:
A Result of Facing Reality

※

Jane Madejczyk, OSF

Introduction

IRENE DUGAN WAS A RELIGIOUS SISTER WHO LOVED GOOD FOOD AND wine, loved music, theater, movies, and books. She had a good eye for quality. She loved a fine fabric and a flattering cut of clothing. She enjoyed celebrations, good restaurants, trips abroad. She had friends who bore no resemblance to each other in terms of lifestyle or points of view. Irene loved to be on the inner grapevine, loved news and to be the source of news for others. She made her preferences known, had no patience with self-pity or passiveness, and was demanding of the best effort . . . first in herself, but also in anyone who presumed to be serious about whatever it was that they were doing. She could listen to an excuse once but set a blue-eyed glare flashing if it showed up again. She was particular and hated settling for less. She loved her family and stayed in close contact with them. Her strong personality attracted both full-hearted friendship and judgmental resentment. Her mind was quick, her laugh was loud and infectious, her voice could be lilting as well as sharp and incisive. She said what she thought. She was interested and engaged.

Many of us who knew Irene describe all of this simply by saying that she loved life. We mean that she had a zest, an energy, a focus to her. We know what it looked like in her, what it felt like. But Irene herself would not be satisfied with looking at "love for life" only from the outside. Knowing this is what led me to reflect on the source of so full an experience of life, what inner work or awareness results in what we call "loving life." I was surprised to come to the conclusion that understanding leads to detachment and detachment leads to love.

I came to know Irene personally in the mid 1980s. She was one of several directors who led a series of annual retreats for a small group of Wheaton Franciscans. Before this time, I was familiar with her only by reputation through friends who knew her quite well through Loyola University and the Institute for Spiritual Leadership. Although I did not have Irene for a director on any of the retreats, we caught each other's eye in conversations and at meals, which were deliciously homemade, not the standard fare. In the late 1980s, Irene moved into a small apartment just a few blocks from where I lived on the north side of Chicago. I asked her if she would be my spiritual director, and she agreed. This relationship proved very satisfying for about a year, until we recognized that we had become genuine friends. The container of spiritual direction no longer fit the relationship, so we decided to abandon it. I found another director, and Irene and I enjoyed the freedom of conversation and expression and the shared intimacies that friends do.

Understanding leads to detachment and detachment leads to love.
Thich Nhat Hanh, a Vietnamese Buddhist monk nominated by Martin Luther King Jr. for the Nobel Peace Prize in 1982, teaches that you cannot love someone or something that you do not understand. Making the effort to understand is necessary for love to be. This effort (he calls it "looking deeply") requires patience, quiet, and attention, and it results in a kind of understanding that is not rational analysis but rather an intuitive knowing. This understanding brings with it satisfaction and relief – an inner experience that comes from learning how pieces fit together, that barriers are false, that apparent contradictions are resolved; the longing to know why is sated.

Looking deeply opens the possibility of seeing someone or some thing apart from ourselves, apart from our own parameters and laws of how things should work. Peace is the fruit of this understanding because we come to see that the particulars of the everyday life we know so well and which get so much of our attention are short-lived and that the meaning we attach to people and events is rooted nearly always in our own neediness or fear. There is nothing lost in coming to this; rather something infinitely more vital is gained. We come to realize, to understand, that there will be clarity and confusion, feast and famine, passion and isolation, that Jesus was right in saying that no one can add one inch to their height or one year to their life by worrying about it (Matthew 6:27).

When we come to understand this, a great burden is surely and gently lifted. It is lifted because the experience of life's transitoriness and illusory meaning, acquired by looking deeply, is accompanied by the experience of a Life within, one that is not governed by any of the changes of the everyday. It is a conscious Presence, steady and inclusive; whole. This is the kingdom of heaven that Jesus spoke about so often, and we discover that it is, as he taught, within. This kind of looking can cause us to take a step or more back, away from what we thought was so. It can become more than a look; it can become a way of seeing this everyday life, a way of understanding, and a way of living it.

Understanding leads to detachment and detachment leads to love.
Detachment is a word that carries baggage from misconstrued notions of asceticism. Rather than disinterested and disengaged, I use it to describe the ability to live without depending on another for identity, the inner personal sense of who I am, for peace of heart, for what our culture defines as happiness. The use of *depend* here is important, because a person who is well developed within will be detached and *therefore* more interested and more engaged in life.

Becoming familiar with the Life within requires the patience, quiet, and attention of looking deeply, but what it brings as a result is an experience of living that is full and intimate, not dependent on position, ownership, or even health. This way of approaching the experience of Life in life is paradoxical, but this is a good and true sign because the wisdom teachings of the world inevitably point to paradox as the key experience of truth. Do we want to experience meaning? belonging? happiness? admiration? love? fullness? security? Then we must let go of the idea that any possession or title, any person, location, job, savings, or achievement is the way to get these. When our attention and effort is directed and distracted toward acquiring, toward holding, toward establishing, toward measuring, we create more distance (and it is an inner distance of the soul) between what we most want and what we have. This is so because we are not meant to spend ourselves in these kinds of efforts. We are not here in this life to establish and protect ourselves. Truly, like Jesus, like the Holy Ones of ages and traditions, we are here to learn and to serve and so to find our way to the sacred. Only seeking the kingdom of heaven within, seeking the Life within life by making a great and consistent effort, can satisfy our heart's desire. This is difficult.

Nothing in our popular culture supports the effort to step away from doing everything it takes to get what we want. Nothing there warns against acquiring and measuring. We are surrounded by every form of urging, counseling, and promising that something in this life can bring us what we want if we have it, do it, use it. Wisdom traditions tell us simply that this is not true, this is not the way. The way is detachment. Detachment, though, is not judgmental and isolating; it does not come from emptiness, but from fullness; it comes from understanding. We are not dependent on what is outside ourselves because we have found what the Gospels call the treasure hidden in the field (Matthew 13:44). That treasure is connection ("union" in the mystic traditions) with the Life within. We recognize Life when we see it and are drawn to it because we are literally related. Our own intimate identity is this conscious Presence; our essence, too, is self-giving, self-expressive.

This is what we have been seeking, and when we have what we seek we see everything differently and we live differently. We do not expect anything or anyone to supply what we know is within ourselves; we do not depend on something outside to make us happy or safe. We do not take our personal sense of identity or measure our value from a possession or an association. We know better. And this knowledge, which is a felt experience, is liberating; it is detachment.

Understanding leads to detachment and detachment leads to love.
In the next breath, after telling us to seek first the kingdom of heaven, Jesus tells us that if we do that, everything else will be given to us besides (Matthew 6:33). What is the "everything"? I believe it is on two levels. The one is whatever we need to live as human beings: nourishment of body, shelter, meaningful work, companionship. But it is also on another level, one where we know harmony, satisfaction, delight,

acceptance, forgiveness, where we know love. Here is the paradox again: if we come to love life by seeking it (the kingdom of heaven, interior and intangible) *first*, then we come to love whatever it is that everyday life brings. This is because when we no longer expect a person or possession to supply something missing, we are able to see the person or the object or the event for what it is in itself, unencumbered by our own neediness. When we can do this, we are able to understand the other, and, going back to Thich Nhat Hanh's teaching, we are able to love. When we are able to enjoy the freedom that detachment brings, we can also enjoy freedom of interest and engagement without the burdens of internalized judgments about what is right or appropriate or timely.

Here is the source of what we commonly describe as a love of life. There is an energy of spirit that enlivens the one who looks deeply; there is a childlike delight, curiosity, ability to trust, to let go, to be grateful. The cliche "What you see is what you get" becomes a lived truth for the one who loves life. It tells us that if we can see beauty or value in whatever it is that presents itself to our awareness, then that is what we get. Of course, the opposite is also true; if we notice nothing, we get nothing. If we see weakness, failure, deformity, or disappointment, then that is what we get. The *Dhammapada,* a compilation of the Buddha's teachings, says something very similar in another way: "We are what we think. All that we are arises with our thoughts. With our thoughts we make the world."

I wonder if the experience of loving life in this way is the "eternal life" that Jesus promised would be the reward of those who "lose this life for the sake of the kingdom" (Matthew 10:39). If we, like Jacob Needleman in his book, *Time and the Soul,* allow "eternal" to mean something very different from the endless duration of linear time, if we allow it to mean an experience of life that is measureless, full, and inclusive, then it is all of a piece.

Understanding leads to detachment and detachment leads to love.

References

There is no more fundamental reference than the perspective and wisdom of Irene Dugan herself. Many conversations with her over several years deeply influence my own sense of where and how to find what is necessary for fullness of life.

Byrom, Thomas, trans. 1993. *Dhammapada: The Sayings of the Buddha.* Boston: Shambhala.

Hanh, Thich Nhat. 1975. *The Miracle of Mindfulness: A Manual on Meditation.* Boston: Beacon Press.

_____. 1990. *Transformation and Healing: The Sutra on the Four Establishments of Mindfulness.* Berkeley, Calif.: Parallax Press.

Kabat-Zinn, Jon. 1994. *Wherever You Go, There You Are: Mindfulness Meditation in Everyday Life.* New York: Hyperion.

Needleman, Jacob. 1998. *Time and the Soul: Where Has All the Meaningful Time Gone? and How to Get It Back.* New York: Doubleday.

Shea, John. 1997–98. *Gospel Food for Hungry People.* Lecture series, Center for Development in Ministry, Mundelein, Illinois.

Scripture references are taken from the Jerusalem Bible.

A Spirituality of Balance

❧

Michael Cooper, SJ

I FIRST MET THIS MUCH TALKED ABOUT "SISTER DUGAN" IN MY FIRST year at the Jesuit School of Theology at Chicago (JSTC). Of all things imaginable, we were taking a course in the Enneagram, offered for the first time ever in the Midwest. Later, I took three retreat and spiritual direction practica from Irene and from Rosemary Duncan, r.c., and in 1973, Irene did the First Reading at my ordination in Cincinnati, staying with my close friends, the Lafkases. In 1975, as a doctoral student in Paris, I welcomed Barbara Howard, Father Larry McBrady, and Irene to a whirlwind tour of "The City of Lights." Dinner in the Latin Quarter over Moroccan wine and couscous remains perhaps the greatest memory of that visit!

Back in the States in 1979, I was able to attend Irene's Golden Jubilee as a Cenacle Sister, and I joined the Wheaton Franciscans at the beautiful Bethany Retreat House in Batavia, Illinois, for several very grace-filled retreats with Irene. Several times she came to the Jesuit Renewal Center to offer her women's retreat, which became such a blessing to many of my own close friends and colleagues in ministry in Cincinnati.

When I moved to Loyola University in 1986, Irene called on me regularly for liturgy and talks for the different groups and classes she taught. With the help of Dr. Tim O'Connell, then the Director of the Institute of Pastoral Studies (IPS), I drew up the proposal and the actual Commendation for Irene's Doctor of Humane Letters *honoris causa*, recognizing the tremendous wisdom and inspiration she had given to so many priests, religious, and laity as well as to the many IPS students whose lives and religious faith had been resurrected through their contact with her.

I look back now in amazement and gratitude at all the things we shared and talked about – God, religious experience, family, Ignatius and the Spiritual Exercises, Progoff, our religious communities and friends, Jung, Rahner, Bernie Siegal, and a whole wealth of wisdom and wonder. I remember fondly those days she seemed to be waiting for me to come in order to share a passage from a book or article she was reading. (She never marked the spot but always seemed to know where to go!) Our involvement in IPS gave us other opportunities to collaborate and share. As long as she was somewhat mobile, Irene always showed up for the end-of-the-semester "Leave Taking" with the students. With equal delight, she always looked forward to the once-a-semester IPS faculty meetings in order to see so many of her close friends whom she did not see as regularly once she started holding her classes at the Cenacle. I was usually her companion in the van that brought her back and forth for these celebrations.

During her last years, when she became more and more confined to the Fullerton Cenacle, I visited Irene every week and was constantly in wonder at how connected she stayed to what was going on in the world religiously, culturally, politically, and every which way! From what we shared and at the depth we shared these precious moments, we were definitely confidants for each other as well as soul friends. Given Irene's great wisdom and holiness, I was always amazed that our relationship remained one of mutuality and equality. She shared as much of her vulnerable self – including her struggles and pains – as I did. For that I am forever blessed and grateful. I was also blessed to be at her bedside along with her sister Nora, her Cenacle Sisters, and other close friends the last days and hours of her earthly journey into God. The length and the breadth, the heights and the depths, of these wonderful memories led me to the following essay.

The great Jesuit theologian Karl Rahner often talked about a "theology of the saints." He believed that the lived and living faith of "saintly" women and men stands as a valid source for understanding the deep truths and wisdom of the Catholic faith. He still held for both the Bible and tradition as sources of revelation, and he did not want to oppose the thematic to the more personal expression of the faith. He did believe, however, that certain "holy" ones capture a unique and vibrant expression of the Christian life. Together, the thematic and the humanly incarnate sources mutually clarify and interpret one another.

Irene loved to read and discuss Rahner when I came to visit her.[1] More than once she told me that when she died she had several questions to pose to Ignatius Loyola about the Spiritual Exercises, and I am sure she had a few questions for Karl Rahner as well. Nonetheless, I believe our Jesuit theologian would agree that our dear friend and companion on the journey, Irene Dugan, a religious of the Cenacle and an extraordinary Christian woman and human being, offers in her life and in her quest into God a very wonderful chapter in *The Theology and Spirituality of the Saints*. No matter our particular community of faith, encounters with Irene called all of us into deeper and wiser explorations of our faith commitments.

Introduction

"A spirituality of balance" can initially sound very ho-hum or superficial – more psychological than spiritual. Balance remains a very popular catchword in business management seminars, self-help books, and so forth. Yet, as I prayerfully reflected over Irene's life, what stood out is her whole sense of balance. Neither formulaic nor superficial, Irene's sense of balance allowed her to embrace so many and at times opposing values and concerns in a tension that was truly creative for her and a gift and a blessing for us to learn from.

Before going on, let me relate a very amusing and also profound incident with Sister Dugan in November 1997. I believe that at the time I was one of the very few who knew that she had cancer. I had stopped by for my usual visit. In the course of our conversation, I mentioned that I was going to Paris over Thanksgiving. I knew how she loved things French from the times she had gone to Paris to give Progoff Journal workshops and renewal retreats for the Cenacle Sisters there. So I asked her what she would like me to bring back from Paris. I thought maybe she might like some brie or some other French cheese or perhaps a bottle of Beaujolais. But no. Irene immediately responded as if she had been waiting for the invitation. "Bouch . . . ." "What's that?" I asked. I did not recognize the word, and Irene was not quite sure how to pronounce it. With that famous Dugan twinkle in her eye and a warm glow on her cheeks, she said, "Perfume!"

At the end of my Thanksgiving stay, I left early for Charles de Gaulle airport outside Paris for my return flight. After checking in, I immediately rushed to the duty-free store on my sacred quest to find Irene's perfume. "Avez-vous un parfum français qui s'appele 'Bouch . . . ou quelque chose com cela?" The saleslady smiled graciously and led me to the Boucheron counter. I was shocked by the price – even in the duty-free store. Suffice it to say that Boucheron was close to the most expensive perfume in the boutique. Irene and I mainly shared books and articles to read and discuss, but we rarely exchanged gifts beyond something simple and symbolic at Christmas or on our birthdays. Since I figured this was probably the last gift I would ever give her, I said what the heck and marched off to the checkout counter. Needless to say, Irene was exceedingly delighted and grateful. She kept it on her nightstand or right inside the drawer until the day she died.

On the surface, this *affaire Boucheron* may seem like no big deal. But for one who knew and loved her from close range, this moment reminded me of how Irene balanced so many apparent opposites – the best and the simplest (she also had simple eau de toilette from the Walgreen's down the street, which she used with equal appreciation), the profound and the ordinary, the latest and the most traditional, for example, her own piety. Irene's "spirituality of balance" held seemingly disparate things together without a lot of exaggeration or compartmentalization. In her, it was all of a piece.

Moreover, her sense of balance was never formulaic – a little of this, a little of that. Neither was her spirit narrow or tight but rather expansive and enthusiastic and thus able to embrace all manner of things in rich diversity. A contemplative look at our friend reveals that this balance, holding such a rich and at times very disparate world of hers together with great spiritual joy and freedom, came from her deep groundedness in her God.

The rest of this essay explores an overview of balance as found in the New Testament, the communitarian spirituality of Benedict, the discernment of spirits of Ignatius Loyola, and the work with dreams and midlife of Carl G. Jung. The reader and friend of Sister Dugan may want to keep her in mind as we meditatively reflect on the "spirituality of balance." The end of the essay highlights some of the more particular applications to Irene's life and ministry as she quested into God.

Balance in the New Testament?

As a quick perusal of any number of biblical dictionaries will make evident, *balance* is not a word found in the New Testament. However, at the end of the "discourse of antitheses," the Beatitudes in Matthew, Jesus sums up all He has just said by exhorting His disciples, "You must, therefore, be *perfect*, just as your heavenly Abba is *perfect*" (Matt. 5:48). Almost always translated as *perfect*, the Greek word *telios* has taken on a strict and demanding tone. For example, do not make any mistakes, always appear correct, and so forth, all the way to a very perfectionistic interpretation such that certain individuals feel driven by their most inhuman and unholy demons to "do the perfect thing," with anything less being a matter of serious sin.

Yet the actual Greek New Testament meaning of *telios* is *whole, complete, balanced!* So Jesus literally summarizes His key message by instructing his disciples: "Be whole, be complete, be balanced in your everyday life for the sake of the Gospel." But what did that mean then, and what does it mean today? It seems so strange to our ears to hear these words coming from Jesus.

Perhaps beginning with the opposites of these words will help. Instead of "whole," unwholesome morally and developmentally, unholy. Instead of "complete," split off, unfinished. Instead of "balanced," exaggerated, off balance.

As the late John L. McKenzie states in his *Dictionary of the Bible*, "More than moral completeness is implied." This coming to full stature, as a human being/disciple of Jesus is "derived from the personal and experiential knowledge of God – not from [observance] of the Law" (1965, p. 651). All of the persevering love and energy for life and ministry comes from a living, personal relationship with God, whose love frees us and challenges us not to hold back. We give ourselves full tilt to our own personal human and religious development while at the same time reaching out in friendship and love to all those who come our way but especially to those in need. Thus, we become whole, complete, and balanced while keeping a discerning eye out for any exaggerations or one-sidedness that may blind us to being open and available in God for whenever and whatever may come our way. Thus, we are called to recognize our Spirit-driven freedom rooted in our friendship with our God. In all of this, a fullness versus an emptiness.

Lest these final words of the Sermon on the Mount remain an individual piety or holiness, Jesus has just spent all the earlier parts of chapter 5 outlining the paradoxical attitudes and values of the reign of God dawning on the planet. For those who can, Jesus invites them to move beyond the taken-for-granted expectations of the world around them and to enter into the mystery and paradox of relationship with God. Concretely, this means moving away from the belief that wealth and success are the signs of God's blessing in order to own their own poverty and need for God. Paradoxically, Jesus proclaims to the *anawim*, who thought they were the forgotten of God who only had time for the wealthy and powerful, that "The Reign of God – this love and power – are really there for you."

The disciples who accept this evangelical relationship also need to recognize the other priorities of paradox and mystery in terms of being gentle, mourning yet somehow already being comforted, hungering and thirsting for justice for themselves and others and finding that very satisfying. Moreover, they feel called to be merciful whether anyone but God knows it or not. And in all this not fleeing persecution or betrayal but letting the reign of God come alive not in spite of but precisely through all of that.

Thus, the centerpiece of Jesus' great discourse comes to mean: Be whole, be complete, be balanced as your heavenly Abba is whole, complete, and balanced. This understanding also avoids tapping into the perfectionism up there. Although it may sound like an anachronism, I believe the fuller meaning of "You must therefore be perfect as your heavenly Abba is perfect" goes something like this: Be all you can be. If you are facing midlife or any other challenging life transition, stay with the process and let me accompany you through till the end, so that you may be whole, complete, and balanced and thus enter into the fullness – not the emptiness – of life. Another gloss on Jesus' saying comes from a paraphrase of Ireneaus the Theologian: "the Glory of God is the human person fully alive." All of this obviously needs to be understood in terms of the apostolic as well as the personal dimensions of the reign of God. And all of this must be lived out in the context of divine paradox and the mystery of God laboring with us and around us.

Thus, Jesus' words in the Gospel have nothing to do with the perfection and perfectionism that can get us Americans so tied up in outer, external voices of guilt and obligation. These very focused works of exhortation challenge us to actualize that *divine balance* which lies at the heart of His gospel call to relationship and to discipleship.

Community for Balance: The Rule of Benedict

When we think of the early forms of religious life, our first thoughts generally call up images of fierce asceticism, unending penances, and a very individualistic pursuit of holiness. As a matter of fact, religious communities early on were referred to in general as "common life" and the Rule served more as a guideline and a manual of spirituality for living in community as the best way known at that time to live the full Christian life and to observe the two great Commandments.

After the Edict of Milan made Christianity the religion of the Roman Empire, some men and women felt that Christianity had become too worldly and lost its challenge for heroic sanctity. As a double protest against the taxation and corruptions of the Roman Empire and the laxity and worldliness of Christianity, individual men and women started to move outside the cities and villages of North Africa and Lower Egypt to the edge of the desert, where they were safe from the Romans but in close enough proximity to villages so that others could come out to them and so that the hermits could enter the villages to sell their wares.

The hermits – male and female – lived alone but never too far from each other, so that they could cry out and be heard in case of threat or illness. Because of the isolation and sensory deprivation, some underwent the equivalent of today's Jungian analysis as their dreams and hallucinations brought their demons and forgotten memories to the surface. Those who survived this descent into their own netherworlds and who were deeply grounded in their own humanity and in their own Christian faith eventually gained renown as wisdom figures. Individuals would come out to the desert to seek spiritual counsel and often stayed for weeks or months as they pursued their own spiritual conversion. Athanasius's *Life of Anthony* is more an exhortation to follow this eremitic life than an actual biography of Anthony.

But not everyone living this solitary life in the desert survived. For some, their own compulsions and perfectionism led to exaggerated forms of asceticism and spiritual practices, so that they ended up with what might be called, for lack of a better name, "spiritual gymnastics" – seeing how many days they could fast or how many days they could survive atop a pillar without coming down, and so on. For others, sensory deprivation, temptations of the flesh, boredom, anxiety, depression, physical privations and excessive penitential watchings, fasts, and prayer combined to destroy the unwary and the proud with frightening ease (cf. Meisel and del Mastro, Introduction, p. 15).

Fear of destruction, mainly self-destruction, threatened to drive the first hermits away. They realized very quickly that, for the majority, living alone without adequate community contact and support allowed their worst compulsions to take over and led to all sorts of imbalances and craziness. For the most part, individuals seemed to stay more balanced living in community. Thus Pachomius, one of the founders of cenobitical life, simply built a wall surrounding all of the huts of his ascetics. They were still pretty much on their own, following their own ascetical programs, but they did meet once a week for spiritual instruction and worship. He also insisted on manual labor performed for the benefit of all. Instead of stifling them, the discipline and order of the "rule" of Pachomius actually freed the hermits to pursue their spiritual agenda.

The value of "common life" as a *sine qua non* for living a balanced life and thus being able to live out the two great Commandments – love of God and love of neighbor – was not lost on the fourth- and fifth-century spiritual leaders like Basil of Caesarea (d. 379) and Augustine of Hippo. Cenobitical life replaced the solitary existence and became the ideal and the model for living the full Christian life. Only the community could meet the necessary needs of both body and soul. Communal living also became the laboratory to learn and exercise fraternal charity while toning down the preoccupation with self. Soon the new members of communities of "common life" realized that the whole was greater than the sum of its parts as the talents, wisdom, and leadership of some helped the others to pursue the Christian ideal of the time. The "common good" took on increasing importance and the abbot or superior understood him- or herself accountable to God not just for the lives of individuals but for their common life together. In other words, the shared life of praying, working, and interacting with one another in community created the necessary environment for safety, spiritual growth, and *balance*.

Benedict of Nursia (480–547 C.E.) created the most effective synthesis of Eastern and Western asceticism in the Europe of the sixth century: Benedict's Rule, which is really a guideline for and exhortation to leading not a superior life but rather a *balanced* life together with others in community. This common life as Benedict envisioned it enabled each individual to achieve the fulfillment of all his potential. It also allowed each one to draw upon the strengths of the others to supply for his weaknesses. This spirit of balance extended to much of monastic life. There was the balance of *Ora et Labora,* between prayer and work. The *Opus Dei,* the formal communal worship, penetrated the monastic day with periods of prayer that was balanced by manual labor.

Benedict's Rule addressed ordinary human beings with both strengths and weaknesses who wanted to live a good Christian life. The Rule took a middle way of balance and common sense. As he says in the prologue to the Rules, "We hope nothing harsh or oppressive will be directed" (Meisel and del Mastro 1975, p. 45). A perhaps exacting but nevertheless apt example of the respect for the individual's human makeup comes in chapter 40 of the Rule, Drink Apportionment:

We hesitate in apportioning other's food. If we are mindful of the sick, a *hemina* (1/4 liter) of wine for each monk each day is adequate we believe.

Depending on local conditions, the strain of labor or excessive heat, more drink may be permitted at the will of the abbot. However, never let drunkenness and excess occur.

We read that wine is not for monks, but in our times they cannot accept this. Let us therefore agree on this limit at least, lest we satiate ourselves with drink. But let us drink temperately.

If circumstances do not permit a full measure (or even any at all), the brothers shall bless God and refrain from complaining.

So we see firsthand Benedict's balance and common sense in facing the humanity of his monks. To paraphrase chapter 40, he seems to say: We have to give the monks their portion of wine. But do not give too much or they will get drunk. Do not give too little, or we will have a riot on our hands!

Thus, we see that one of the great gifts of the early forms of common life, and the Benedictines in particular, lies not just in their ascetical practices but also in their communitarian spirituality. Whether we are in a formal religious group or not, we are reminded that we each and all need community. The early pioneers realized only too well that people living isolated and apart from community have a tendency to become a little exaggerated, a little crazy. We each need some community to which we belong and in which we are loved and appreciated for who we are. In real communities, whatever form they take, the individual almost by necessity has to balance some of his or her own preoccupations with the needs of the others around them. In community, we are stretched as we try to appreciate and not just tolerate people different from ourselves. We cannot get away from them! Our weaknesses, as Benedict mentioned, are balanced by others' strengths. Moreover, in these days when stress and burnout remain so evident all around us, the Benedictine charism challenges us to balance our *ora* and our *labora* – our prayer and work – and thus to be really human!

Luckily, this communitarian spirituality is surfacing all over – in the small Christian communities of faith sharing in the RENEW program in parishes, the *communidad de base* in Central and Latin America. Even my very activist community, the Jesuits, continues to recognize the need and value of being "friends in the Lord" and not just business associates sharing the same address!

Balance for Discernment

The Spiritual Exercises of Saint Ignatius Loyola have as their purpose:

> preparing and disposing our soul to rid itself of all its disordered affections and then ... of seeking and finding God's will in the ordering of our life for the salvation of our soul. (SPEX 1)[2]

Although the sixteenth-century formulation may sound a bit stiff and philosophical, the Exercises offer an unfolding process to find interior *balance* and *spiritual freedom*. The person making the Exercises (the exercitant or retreatant) can, with God's help, discover God's dream for him or her, that is, discover the true self in relationship to the true God and then the best way of living out that dream and service. In this short essay, we cannot summarize the whole dynamic of the Exercises but just highlight the importance of balance as an expression of true spiritual freedom. This balance lets the exercitant place him- or herself freely in God's hands, so that God can work with them to discover what is best for the individual in order to love God and serve the neighbor in deep peace and joy.

Ignatius opens the Exercises with the "Principle and Foundation" (SPEX 23), a consideration of the sacred destiny of each one, the importance of using created things to help in attaining that destiny. Ignatius ends by suggesting the cultivation of a disposition of *indifference* regarding created things:

> Consequently on our part we are not to seek health rather than sickness, wealth rather than poverty, honor rather than dishonor, a long life rather than a short one, and so in all matters. (SPEX 23)

This indifference has been hard to understand. In the Exercises, it means keeping a balance and not leaning towards one thing or the other, being really open to seeking and finding God and God's hopes and dreams no matter what comes one's way. This disposition also allows God complete openness so that God can uncover whatever is the truest and best for the individual and for the service of the reign of God. Initially, Ignatius offers this as a consideration while the rest of the process of the Exercises helps one come to that balance and poised freedom to follow God's workings within.

It should be noted that the director does not try to influence the exercitant's eventual discernment or decision. In his introductory comments, Ignatius counsels the guide to remain "standing like the pointer of a scale in equilibrium" (SPEX 15) so that the Creator can deal directly with the Creature and the Creature directly with the Creator.

The First Week or movement invites the person to explore his or her sins and weaknesses and the sins and weaknesses of family, culture, and world that can take away spiritual freedom and balance. The retreatant comes to know that he or she is loved as they are, even as a sinner. They no longer have to hide their true selves from God or from themselves.

One person recently described this process as "repenting of my excuses." For some, this conversion of the First Week is sufficient. Others want to place their whole lives in God's hands and so continue on in the Second Week contemplating the public life and ministry of Jesus. Discernment of spirits regarding a life choice or other significant issues begins during this time. Discernment always takes place in terms of the ongoing Gospel and the decision to follow Christ ever more closely in relationship but also on mission – the apostolic side.

Ignatius offers Rules for Making an Election (SPEX 169–189) and Rules for Discernment of Spirits (SPEX 313–336). The most important rule is number 179. After a repeat of the dispositions of the principle and foundation, Ignatius reminds the retreatant not to preplan or program his/her choices:

> I ought to find myself indifferent, that is, without any disordered affections to such an extent that I am not more inclined or emotionally disposed toward taking the matter proposed rather than relinquishing it, nor more toward relinquishing it than taking it. Instead, I should find myself in the middle, *like the pointer on a balance.*

We see that great and deep spirit of balance rooted in the depth of oneself and opened out toward God's working, however God wishes to help the exercitant discover the dream – the best of me for God and the service of the neighbor. Karl Rahner has developed this point in terms of "God's individual, particular will that has no a priori's." Thus we see where true spiritual balance goes – a developing process growing to more and more openness and freedom in God. "It cannot get much better than that!"

The Third and Fourth Weeks contemplating the passion, death, and resurrection of Jesus give the exercitant the courage and strength to live this mystery. Ignatius closes the Exercises with the Contemplation to Attain Love, where we find the *Suscipe* that expresses these dispositions as the ongoing fruit of the Exercises – the balance and freedom thus to "find God in all things":

> Take, Lord, and receive all my liberty, my memory, my understanding, and all my will – all that I have and possess. You have given all that to

me. I now give all back to You, O Lord. All is yours. Dispose of it according to Your will. Give me love of Yourself along with your Grace, for that is enough for me. (SPEX 234)

Dreams of Balance

Other contributors to this book in honor of Irene are developing at length themes tied to Ira Progoff and Carl Jung. Before concluding though, I want to emphasize the whole psychology of balance at work in dreams and in midlife. Dreams function to bring balance to our psyche – to bring out hidden or unnoticed parts of ourselves that God, the Dream Maker, feels are ready to see the light of day and to work for us, precisely in coming to more balance! So too the midlife journey becomes a very focused time to allow that self-balancing to come about. My basic identity has solidified and now I am ready to welcome the other parts of me that did not have a chance in the first part of my life.

Tribute

In this final section, I would like to talk about my dear friend Irene. I do not intend to make every application possible between her life and the overview of balance I have given above. Maybe it is enough if we recognize that Irene kept a tremendous balance at equilibrium that in part made her the unforgettable person she was and is. Maybe, too, this essay encourages each of us to take our own spirituality of balance seriously and allow Irene to be a saintly model for us.

"Be whole, be complete, be balanced as your heavenly Abba is." Any of us who knew Irene in class, on retreat, in conversation, or wherever were constantly amazed at the sources she read or quoted or the new twists on old ideas or the wonderful creations of her own divine wisdom. Irene could surprise, perhaps shock, some because she really followed this gospel dictum to keep growing and living the paradoxes and mysteries of life. Irene took seriously Jesus' desire that she grow and grow and grow, and all the while keeping things in balance.

At the heart of her quest was her living relationship with God – her rock and fortress amid all the pain of becoming more and more immobile. Many people are surprised to learn that Irene considered herself an introvert. Yet she had that deep well where she went down to her

God who waited for her. This relationship allowed her to live life as one piece, holding all things together. Her love relationship was the secret of her balance at equilibrium. Occasionally I would hear her jokingly refer to her "bum leg," which kept her dependent on others for essential needs. Certainly there were frustrating moments but they never got the best of her. She kept her balance. She acknowledged the inconvenience and occasionally decried the lack of care for all the elderly sisters, but I never heard her complain about her lot. Her very real relationship with God gave her deep freedom and helped her keep her balance.

Her spirituality was always expansive and exuberant. One day, in her later years, she asked me to get her a set of tarot cards from the Jung Center. Personally, these sorts of things are not my cup of tea! Irene wanted to explore them. Her spirituality and grounded relationship with the Lord let her do that. This incident also serves as a reminder of her experiential wisdom and grounded balance. Everything held in place. Her friend, whom she read frequently, Teilhard de Chardin, said it well: "Nothing is profane for those who have eyes to see."

Irene was very much a community person and really made efforts to stay connected to people despite her growing immobility. What I find deeply significant in regard to community is that Irene tried to never to work alone but always in collaboration with other friends and colleagues. I remember women's retreats where Irene asked Margie Perzynski, Maureen McGrath, or Avis Clendenen to join her, another example of balance and equilibrium where she invited others to "balance" out the program. At JSTC, she taught her retreat practica with Rosemary Duncan, r.c., and also with Paul Robb, SJ. Moreover, although I heard some people refer to it as Irene's group, I never remember Irene referring to it as anything other than "the women's group." To her, it was a community thing.

Sister Dugan also had that Franciscan spirit that respected creation and rejoiced in her own humanity. She could enjoy a glass of fine wine or the scent of Boucheron. When these good things of the earth were there, she enjoyed them. When they were not, she enjoyed whatever else was there in that rich spirit of balance.

Irene was a tremendous spiritual director. She continued to teach her course on the Exercises into her last years. I see now that each time she taught them they were a deepening of her own balance and spiritual freedom, so she could make the *Suscipe* or Mere Terese Couderc's prayer of surrender. God had truly found Irene in all the elements of her life – gifts and blessings, health and illness. Irene leaves us a legacy of deep spiritual balance, which we realize now is another word for *freedom in the Spirit*.

In teaching and in direction, Irene was a strong and forceful wisdom figure. She was fully engaged in our growth and development, yet she always let "the Creator deal directly with the Creature and the Creature directly with the Creator." Through all she lived, celebrated, and also suffered, she knew from the inside God's individual particular will and dream for her, and she respected that process in her students and directees. The proof of that comes in the rich diversity of people who came to her – ordinary people, extraordinary people, gifted people, wounded people – all of God's people.

Rahner was right. We can learn a lot about the foundations of the Christian faith from the saints. As I said my last good-bye to Irene the evening she went to God, I took the bottle of Boucheron from her nightstand and dabbed a little on her sacred humanity. I kissed her and handed the Boucheron to Irene's sister Nora, sitting by her bed, and said, "Take this. Irene would want you to have this." May the perfume of Irene's sanctity, freedom, and balance continue to challenge us. Thank you, my dear friend. Saint Irene, pray for us!

Notes

1. Karl Rahner remains one of the greatest theologians of the twentieth century and the architect of several major decrees of Vatican II; he, along with Father General Pedro Arrupe, SJ, renewed Ignatian and Jesuit spirituality on an international level.

2. SPEX refers to the numbered paragraphs in the text of the Exercises.

References

Loyola, I. 1992. *The Spiritual Exercises of Saint Ignatius Loyola*. Chicago: Loyola Press.

McKenzie, J. L. 1965. *Dictionary of the Bible*. Milwaukee: Bruce Publishing.

Meisel, A., and del Mastro, M. 1975. *The Rule of Saint Benedict*. Garden City, N.Y.:Doubleday.

Rahner, K. 1966. *The Dynamic Element in the Church*. New York: Herder and Herder.

The Discernment of Life Tasks in the Progoff Intensive Journal Process

※

Joyce Kemp, r.c.

Introduction

I RENE DUGAN WAS MY SPIRITUAL DIRECTOR AND MENTOR FOR MANY years, first when we lived together at the Longwood Cenacle in the Morgan Park area of Chicago, and then at the Cenacle on Fullerton Parkway. I found her both supportive and challenging. She introduced me to the Intensive Journal process of Dr. Ira Progoff when I first moved to the Longwood Cenacle. In fact, she brought him to Chicago in the 1970s to give workshops at our house. When Longwood became too small for the hundreds attending his workshops, he moved to Loyola University and then to DePaul University. I participated in a ten-day workshop led by Sister Dugan and an English Jesuit, Bill Hewitt, in June 1980 that changed my life. They combined the Life Context and Depth Contact Intensive Journal workshops with a life study of St. Ignatius of Loyola using the Progoff methods. On the ninth day, I experienced a spiritual awakening as I worked with a dream that I had had when I was eleven or twelve years old. I felt as though I had reconnected with my soul. After the workshop, Irene asked to speak with me. She told me that she was getting old and asked if I would be willing to follow in her footsteps. I was honored to do so and began preparing to become an Intensive Journal consultant. I led my first workshop in Kansas City, Missouri, in the fall of 1982.

The Intensive Journal Process

"I wish God would send me a letter and tell me what to do," young adults in our contemporary world say with a deep sigh. Several hundred years ago, such a thought would never have occurred to most people. Women married and bore children. Men did what their fathers had done before them. Place in society and life task were givens for almost everyone. Today, those in first-world countries are presented with myriad possibilities in life. We can't be and do everything that presents itself, so we are faced with choosing this rather than that. We are thrown back upon ourselves to discern who we are, why we are here, and what our life's purpose is. We ask, along with Parker J. Palmer, whether the life we are living is the same as the life that wants to live in us (Palmer 2000, p. 2).

The Intensive Journal process, developed by Ira Progoff over a twenty-five-year period beginning in the late 1950s, provides an instrument and a method for discerning the direction of the movement of one's life and how it wants to unfold. The Intensive Journal process invites us to go inward and pay attention to the constant stream of images that flows in our depths: memories, inspirations, and perceptions. By tapping into the deeper-than-conscious layers of the psyche, bringing what is there to conscious awareness and recording what comes to us, we are able to recapture what has been going on in our depths each time we reread our entries.

Since the images in the deeper-than-conscious layers of our psyche are symbolic in form, they may not give us instant direction. They are like dream material, calling our attention to some aspect of our life: our relationships with people, our body, events, circumstances, work, and society.

Underlying Progoff's approach to journal work is the understanding that we come into the world with certain seeds of potential coded in our beings. When the growth of any of these seeds is frustrated, we manifest symptoms of physical, mental, emotional, or spiritual malaise. Healing comes from going inward and bringing to the surface our deepest heart's desire. Progoff went beyond the medical model of psychoanalysis in his approach. The medical model diagnoses the cause of symptoms and then prescribes a cure. Progoff's approach is "psyche-evoking." Through the Intensive Journal process we are able to go into our depths and find seed-images of unlived potential. The seed-images that have not had an opportunity to germinate and grow contain blocked energy that causes us to feel frustrated, confused, or depressed. It is by releasing the energy of the seed-image and manifesting it in the outer world that the symptoms of pathology are overcome. Progoff compared the evocation of the psyche to psychoanalysis using the image of a boulder in a stream. The psychoanalyst chips away at the boulder that impedes the flow of the stream. The evocation of psyche, on the other hand, simply raises the level of the water so that it runs around and over the boulder (Progoff 1985, pp. 248–249).

There are many ways to move inward in the Intensive Journal. One is to sit in a quiet atmosphere, enter into a twilight state of consciousness somewhere between waking and sleeping, pay attention to what we behold there, and record it in a neutral, noninterpretive, and nonjudgmental way. The series of images recorded over time provides the source for a variety of active Journal Feedback exercises. Another similar source is the record of a series of sleeping dreams.

A third method for going inward is the Entrance Meditation. Progoff published three books of Entrance Meditations over a period of ten years. The first, *The Well and the Cathedral*, grew out of his fascination with a spiritual classic, *The Cloud of Unknowing*, written by an anonymous fourteenth-century monk. Progoff translated it into contemporary English so that it would speak to today's readers. Even then, he felt the symbols did not speak to our experience. The symbols he used in his Entrance Meditations came from his own inner work in the Intensive Journal process. They were chosen as metaphors that would help a person move inward: the shaft of a well leading to an underground stream, a long dark corridor leading to an underground chapel, and a forest whose trees leave no space for sunlight to come through. Each series of Entrance Meditations invites us to focus on our breath, allowing it to find its own pace. As we do that, we move inward to a place of quiet where our body relaxes, our thoughts come to rest, and our self becomes still. The meditations continue, inviting us to look at the cycles and phases of our life and of all life throughout history. They move from the personal to the transpersonal. The presenter reads the meditation, suggesting images rather than allowing them to emerge spontaneously. The purpose of the entrance meditation is to act as a mediator between the inner and the outer, the surface and the depths. It leads us inward without the introduction of any special doctrine or set of beliefs. The images that come to us are recorded in a section called the Meditation Log.

The fourth way Progoff created to move inward is the Mantra Crystal meditation. When he introduced this in his book, *The Practice of Process Meditation,* published in 1980, interest in the use of the mantra in this country was still new. He differed from such schools as transcendental meditation by suggesting that we create our own mantra, a seven-syllable phrase that crystallizes our past, our present, and our future in a single statement. It is not to be a complete sentence, as its purpose is to draw us into the true unfolding of our life.

Once we find a phrase that meets all of his criteria, we sit in stillness, letting our breath become slower and softer. When we are ready, we begin to say the mantra under our breath, repeating it over and over until the rhythm of the breath and the beat of the mantra fit together and support each other. As we continue to repeat the mantra crystal, we move to a silence beyond ego-consciousness, allowing the deepest parts of the twilight range of our being to open themselves to us. We record what is shown to us there as it comes to us, an exercise that takes a little practice. Eventually, we find ourselves able to write without having to leave the depths of the twilight level. The intuitions, perceptions, and memories that come to us serve as a springboard to further work in the Journal. A question we ask whenever we finish recording is, "To what aspect of my life is this calling my attention?" Then we list places in our Journal where we might begin our active Journal Feedback work (there are four main dimensions and twenty-two major sections).

Writing Our Life

What might we find in our depths? Buried treasures? Scary monsters? Memories we'd just as soon forget? Whatever lies there represents a road not taken in life. Progoff provides two places in his Journal to explore these roads. The first, Intersections, appears in the Time/Life Dimension, a place that allows us to move back and forth through the segments of both chronological and qualitative time in our existence. It allows us to look at the outer embodiment of the inner process of our lives. Chronological time refers to the objective observation of a sequence of events outside of oneself. Qualitative time, on the other hand, is about the subjective perception of objective events in terms of the inner meaning and value they have for the person who is experiencing them. The second section, Re-openings, is in the Meaning Dimension and addresses spiritual roads not taken. Both are connected to and follow another exercise called the "Steppingstones" of our lives. Steppingstones are those key events that come to us spontaneously in the present moment as we look back over our life in a waking dream state. The first Steppingstone in the Time/Life Dimension is free. "I was born, and then . . . ." We record whatever comes to us spontaneously, from the depths of our psyche. Each Steppingstone represents a period of our life. As we write about the Steppingstone periods in our life, we begin to see things we might have done or become but did not because of unforeseen circumstances or our own choices. Those that still hold promise for future unfolding are recorded and explored. We place ourselves back in those times that were points of transition, where a change of some sort became inevitable. We recognize that our choices then left many potentialities untouched and unexplored. They are capacities of life that were bypassed. The energy and potential for the expression of these capacities are waiting for the right time and the right circumstances to emerge. In Intersections, life tasks might be the focus. In Re-openings, we look for unlived potential in the spiritual history listed in our Spiritual Steppingstones – all the ways we have searched for what is true and meaningful in our life.

Once we have recorded the capacities that have gone unlived in our life, we ask, "Is the time to express them now? Shall I express my seed potential in the same way today as I might have earlier in life? How does my life want to unfold?" We explore these questions further in other sections of the Journal. For example, we might enter into a dialogue with something creative we wanted to do but put off. If thinking about it still excites us and gives us energy, it may be a seed that needs to be planted. It does not have to be a great work of art. It might be something as fulfilling as gardening or decorating a room.

Our life task, the potential for being a poet, an entrepreneur, an engineer, or a politician, is present in us from the very beginning. A good question to ask ourselves when we are looking for seed-images is,

"What fascinated me when I was a child?" Einstein was enchanted with magnets. Virginia Woolf was captivated by waves. I loved playing with my chemistry set. Perhaps you gathered the children in your neighborhood together to put on a play. These early interests often manifest themselves throughout our lives. I did not become a chemist, but I did become interested in the process of spiritual transformation. Progoff called our tendencies of individual expression *dynatypes*. Archtypes are universal patterns of energy. Dynatypes are more personal energy patterns. They flow from our true identity, not what those around us want us to be or to do. Once we connect with our true self and know who we are, we can discover what course our life is to take and what our life task is. Because we live much longer than our ancestors did, it is possible to pursue more than one life task over time. Albert Schweitzer, for example, was a musician, a theologian, and a medical doctor who became a missionary in Africa.

Progoff built the structure of his Intensive Journal on his study of the lives of creative people. He wanted to enable ordinary people to enter into the same process he found in the lives of highly creative people such as Dostoyevsky and Pablo Casals. What he discovered was that great artists had the capacity to mediate between their outer work and their inner resources, between the surface of their lives and their depths. In the case of an author, just the right word comes unbidden. Fiction writers will tell you that at a certain point, their books take on lives of their own and write themselves through their hands and their pens (or typewriters, or computers). Progoff compared this creative process to the Psalms. The psalmist cries out, "How long, O Lord?" as he describes a difficult situation. Then, as he bemoans his difficulties, the atmosphere changes, and he ends with a song of praise. The psalmist has moved down to his depths and has returned reconnected to his essence.

Attending to the Inner and Outer Dialogue

Our essence is the person within the process of the movement and unfolding of our life – that thread of a special and unique continuity in the series of inner and outer events we have experienced. When we work in the Journal, we place ourselves in the movement of our life as a whole. Progoff referred to Henri Bergson's sense of getting an inner perspective of our life when speaking of this process. The Journal is not so much about what happened *to us,* as it is about what happens *in us.* For this reason, as we work in the movement our life, we begin to see it from another point of view. New understandings lead to new feelings and new behaviors. When I was a senior in high school, a member of the Milwaukee Symphony told me I would be an excellent accompanist. I felt insulted. I wanted to be a concert pianist and that was that. When I realized my goal in life was unobtainable, I quit. Many years later, I realized that this man had paid me a great compliment. It is much more difficult to accompany another musician than it is to play a solo. Just recently, I was accompanying a lyric soprano on the piano. I enjoyed working with her immensely. I realized then that a change in my attitude toward being an accompanist had resulted in a change of my feelings about it as well.

Ira Progoff created the Intensive Journal to fill a void he saw in the modern world. It lacked a spiritual discipline that not only enabled us to make contact with our depths but also helped us to draw guidance from them in a systematic way. The Journal Process begins with the collection of raw data about our inner and outer life experiences. Once we have collected the raw data, we move to active work with his Journal Feedback exercises in order to reach greater felt realizations. We cannot see our life in its entirety without beginning to notice emerging patterns that are not unique to us. Many who have gone before us have had similar experiences. We can learn from them by entering into a dialogue process.

The Dialogue dimension of the Journal is one of the key Journal Feedback processes of Progoff's method. A dialogue is more than a written conversation between two people. A deep inner relationship between the two has to be established first – the I-Thou relationship of which Martin Buber, the great Jewish philosopher, wrote. Two persons speak and listen, essence to essence. Their meeting is one of mutuality, depth speaking to depth. The quality of this deep inner relationship enables the varied mini-processes of our individual existences to change and move and develop in relation to each other. The major goal of this method is to establish an encompassing dialogue between our inner self and the whole unfolding movement of our life (Progoff 1992, pp. 125–126).

The written script does not begin until we have placed ourselves in the present moment of our life and have described where we stand in relationship to the person with whom we are about to dialogue. Once we have written a brief opening statement regarding this relationship, we move to the writing of the Steppingstones of the other person *as though we were this person.* Of course, we need to know the person we have chosen well enough to do this. We write in the first person, beginning with "I was born." This exercise in itself can be very powerful, for we begin to see life from the other person's point of view as well as our own.

Once we have completed the set of Steppingstones, we move into that twilight place somewhere between being wide awake and fully asleep. In the stillness, we feel the movement of our life, and we feel the movement of the other person's life. We allow twilight images to arise, and we record them just below the list of Steppingstones. Staying in this place, we move into the presence of the other person. We feel him or her present with us now. We meet with each other beyond our usual level of repetitious arguments and worn-out conversations. We are in a new place, speaking to one another in a totally unconditional way. We begin the dialogue by greeting each other. We may refer to something that was written in our opening statement or we may ask a burning question. We record in our Journal whatever we say. We listen to the other's responses and record them. On this deep level of consciousness, we allow the dialogue to continue, writing itself as it were, through our pen. We do not force or control it any more than we do our dreams. The principle at play in the psyche here is the same as in sleeping dreams. Our psyche selects and presents symbolic material that is relevant to our life here and now. As our dialogue script comes to a close, we return to stillness. We pay attention to any strong emotions stirring in us and take note of them. Then we read the dialogue script back to ourselves. In a workshop atmosphere, participants are invited to do this aloud. Reading aloud evokes stronger emotions and perceptions than rereading in silence. Those who are working alone can experience the same evocation of further experiences by reading the script into a cassette recorder and listening to it afterwards. Whatever occurs is recorded at the bottom of the dialogue script.

Dialoguing with another person who has an inner significance to us may help us clarify what we are being called to in life. A more effective place to dialogue when trying to discern our life task, however, is in the Dialogue with Works. The word *work* in the Intensive Journal does not refer to a job. It refers to a specific and tangible task, a creative work of art that is the external manifestation of an inner vision. This work of art does not have to be in the fine arts or literature. It may be in any field – science, philosophy, or sports, for example. Our ultimate work of art is our own life.

In the section of Dialogue with Works, we list those activities that carry a lot of energy with them, projects in which we have a special interest. Then we choose one as a dialogue partner. We follow the same procedure as for the Dialogue with Persons. The only difference is that now we are dialoguing with the person who lives within the life of the work of art. We begin by describing the work we have chosen and our relationship to it.

Dennis is a young man torn between a career his parents chose for him and his true calling.

> From the time I was a little boy, I have loved to play the piano. I started taking lessons before I learned how to read words. It has been my passion. My parents discouraged me from making the piano my career. They said that they would pay my college tuition only if I agreed to study dentistry. I am now in my fifth year of dental school and will graduate in a few months. The piano is still what gives me joy. I don't want to be a dentist. I am going to dialogue with playing the piano to see what it has to say to me.

Next he lists the Steppingstones of the person who exists within the life of playing the piano in the first person. He might write: "I began when Dennis was three and picked out 'Twinkle, Twinkle, Little Star' on the piano." Then he lists whatever events in its life come to him next. When he completes his list, he moves into stillness to behold and record whatever twilight imagery surfaces. Our dental student might record images of times when he was playing the piano and the joy he felt. He might record feelings of repugnance toward becoming a dentist. We limit the number of Steppingstones to ten or twelve in order to force our psyche to be more selective, presenting only those events that are relevant to where we are in our life here and now. When the list is complete, we return to stillness, close our eyes and enter into the twilight level of consciousness. We record whatever comes to us as we move into the presence of the person living within the work of art we have chosen.

When Dennis is ready, he comes into the presence of the person in the life of playing the piano and greets it.

Dentist: Hello, my old friend.

Piano: Hello. I've missed feeling your fingers on my keys every day.

Dentist: I've missed you, too. All I've ever wanted to do is play you, and to teach others, too.

Piano: Then why did you abandon me?

Dentist: I wanted to go to college, and my parents wouldn't pay my tuition to study you.

Piano: You could have found other ways to continue studying me. For example, seeking a scholarship or working part-time.

Dentist: I guess I didn't consider that five years ago. Now it's too late. I could make a lot of money as a dentist, but I don't think I'd be happy.

Piano: Money doesn't make people happy. Doing what they love and living with meaning does.

Dentist: So what should I do?

Piano: Think about giving up dentistry and playing me instead.

Dentist: I suppose I could get a job playing in nightclubs and studying during the day.

Piano: That sounds like a good idea to me.

The dental student would then sit quietly, record whatever came to him as he was writing in terms of emotions, and then reread the dialogue and record what else is evoked, for example, a surge of energy when he thinks of pursuing his dream or fear at the thought of telling his parents. Whenever something has a strong emotional impact on us, we know that it has an inner importance for the movement of our lives.

Insight and Empowerment

As Dennis continues working in the Intensive Journal process, he experiences the movement of his life from a broader perspective and is able to move beyond the emotions of the moment. He may see, for example, that he has been trying to please his parents rather than listening to his own desires. He may realize that he is not the only person caught between the wishes of parents and one's true calling in life. Getting in touch with larger-than-personal patterns takes us out of our immediate and individual situation and enables us to see it with greater clarity and inner freedom. We may feel stuck in a situation, for example, until we discover that there is more than one way to look at it and there are many options for moving ahead.

When we begin to explore our seed potential using the Intensive Journal method, we are like muddy water. Our mind and emotions are stirred up and full of thoughts, images, and feelings. By sitting in stillness, the mud settles to the bottom, and the surface of the water becomes like a mirror, reflecting images back to us with greater clarity. Further work in the Intensive Journal enables us to see our life and its various aspects from more than one point of view. We begin to perceive that we are participating in patterns that transcend our individual lives. We are not the first to pass this way, nor will we be the last. By tapping into the energy of the unlived potential of our lives, we are able to move forward with an inner authority and freedom from outside pressures. We are convinced that the next step we are to take in life is the one that has presented itself to us intuitively from the depths of our being.

References

Palmer, Parker J. 2000. *Let Your Life Speak: Listening for the Voice of Vocation.* San Francisco: Jossey-Bass, Inc., Publishers.

Progoff, Ira. 1992. *At a Journal Workshop: Writing to Access the Power of the Unconscious and Evoke Creative Ability.* Los Angeles: Jeremy P. Tarcher, Inc.

_____. 1957. *The Cloud of Unknowing.* New York: Delta Publishing Co., Inc.

_____. 1985. *The Dynamics of Hope.* New York: Dialogue House Library.

_____. 1980. *The Practice of Process Meditation: The Intensive Journal® Way to Spiritual Experience.* New York: Dialogue House Library.

_____. 1963. *The Symbolic and the Real.* New York: McGraw-Hill, 1973.

_____. 1971. *The Well and the Cathedral: An Entrance Meditation.* New York: Dialogue House Library.

No Shortcuts to the Promised Land: Creating Character from Crises

‌⁂

Avis Clendenen

Preface

I NO LONGER REMEMBER EXACTLY WHAT OCCASIONED OUR LENGTHY foray into the biblical character of Moses, but my spiritual guide, Sister Irene Dugan, r.c., and I seemed to spend considerable time probing the legendary saga of Moses. While on an eight-day retreat in the late 1970s I returned to the theme of Moses again, and Irene mentioned a manuscript that Dr. Ira Progoff had given her to read. The text was titled "Moses and God."[1] I vividly remember her sharing with me facets of her interesting relationship with Ira Progoff, the creator of the Intensive Journal Program, the practices of Process Meditation™, and the founder of Dialogue House in New York. Apparently Irene had had a recent encounter with Ira, who expressed to her that he thought she was a "very wise old woman and a very wise old man." At that time, Irene was near seventy and I was in my late twenties. I knew that Ira had offered Irene an important gift in so naming her both a wise woman and a wise man. I knew that in sharing Ira's comment with me she was instructing me about the path of integration. I had a sense of the importance of this lesson, although I didn't quite comprehend its prophetic wisdom at the time. I wanted to read Progoff's manuscript. Initially Irene said no. I continued the retreat, and a few days later Irene handed me "Moses and God." She said bluntly, "You have twenty-four hours. I want this back in my hands by tomorrow afternoon." Irene and

I related on a dramatic level, so I was all the more interested in probing its pages, knowing that Irene had some hidden hesitancy about my reading the manuscript.

Over the decades, the character and crises of Moses have remained for me an enigmatic and compelling source of spiritual insight, nurture, and challenge. Such is true as well of Sister Irene Dugan. The wise old men and wise old women emerge and prompt considerations about the quest for human and spiritual wholeness, limits and possibilities, infinite potentialities and terrorizing finitude, the interplay of light and shadow, and the mystery and misery of the pilgrimage we call life.

Introduction: The Bible as Permanently Meaningful Source

The Hebrew and Christian scriptures are a cornucopia of literature, history, geography, archeology, anthropology, linguistics, origins of religion, revelatory faith, myth, and symbol. For those who claim the Book sacred, the Bible holds, enfolds, and unfolds incomprehensible mystery and permanent meaning. It is, as theologian David Tracy describes, a classic religious text. One approaches this permanently meaningful text with a deep consciousness of its history and, at the same time, a radical openness to its revelatory timelessness. It is a book that never fades in memory. Its power does not subside. Every classic text lives as such only if it finds readers and listeners willing to be provoked by its claim to attention (Tracy 1986, p. 102). Once claimed, the possibility of an encounter follows whereby the hearer of the word is engaged, challenged, illumined, transformed. This is the normative nature of a truth-telling text. It also suggests that a truly classic text, such as the Bible, is a dynamic encounter, even a risk-taking event. Opening oneself to a meeting with biblical memory, one might say, triggers an engagement in the reader or hearer of the word in such a way as to actually induce a change in understanding, a *metanoia*.[2] In short, "what we mean in naming certain texts, events, images, rituals, symbols, and persons 'classics' is that here we recognize nothing less than the disclosure of a reality we cannot but name truth" (ibid., p. 108).

In the search for truth, the field of biblical criticism requires well-honed skills in the scholarship and art of exegesis and hermeneutics. The issues of historical context, authorship, authenticity, verifiability, genre, audience, and a score of other questions guide the interpretive scholar in scrutinizing the text and its demand for constant interpretation. The scholarly exegetical analyses of the Book of Exodus is not, however, the approach that will be applied in this essay to the timeless truth – the classicness – of the biblical Moses, who is an exemplar of a wise old man and a wise old woman. Whatever the mixture of fact and legend in the biblical narrative, the indwelling story of faith remains authentic. The words of the Book of Exodus become the voice of the personalities of Moses and God. The power of the ancient Moses lies in the power of the sacred story to affect us today. Thus, this essay is an exercise in narrative theology and depth psychology where the mythic stories are told to see how they render reality in a new way. Indeed, without attending to classic narratives we cannot fully understand the cultural range of health and pathology available to us. We are relational beings; stories that shape us are "narrative transactions" that carry enduring power for growth in the here and now (Brueggemann 1990, p. 43). The reader is invited into the narrative daring of the old story where there is a chance that through this rendering we shall meet God face to face.

Midrash on Moses

A midrash is a Hebrew text using biblical legends to teach life lessons. Midrash does not address precise relations to biblical text. Midrashim are rich in talmudic interpretations, parables, similes, and sayings. The tellers of these tales weave their stories to "quicken" the souls of the hearers so that the story is an avenue bringing the community of listeners and disciples to deeper communion in spirit and in truth. The following is a paraphrase of a more than five-hundred-year-old midrash arising from the Kurdistani Jews (Gerstein 1994; Wiesel 1976, pp. 174–205; Ginzberg 1998, pp. 431–81).

It is told that when Moses reached the age of a hundred and twenty, God led him up to the top of Mount Nebo and said, "Look! Before you lies the land of milk and honey. The land that I promised to you and your people."

"At last," said Moses. "How I've longed to see it."

"Look well," said God, "but sadly you shall not go there. Your life has reached its end. Now your soul must return to me."

"But Lord," said Moses, "why now? Give me a little longer. My hundred and twenty years seems like one short day."

"A man or woman's life," said God, "is like the shadow of a flying bird. Even if you lived a thousand years, at the end it would seem but one day. Your time has come."

Then Moses stood up and began to pray that he might live. Moses prayed five hundred and fifteen prayers and sent them to heaven. "Lock the doors and windows," said God, "the prayers of Moses may not enter. His time has come."

"Oh Lord of the world," said Moses, "let me be a fish of the sea or a sheep that eats grass on the hill. Only let me live."

"Everything born has a time to die," said God. I cannot change that."

"Dear Lord!" cried Moses. "Turn me into a butterfly; I'd eat nothing and I'd sleep on the wind. Just let me live!"

And God said to the angel Gabriel, "Go down, fetch the soul of Moses and bring it home." Three times did the angel move toward Moses yet was powerless to do anything but look at him from afar. "Enough!" said God. "Moses, prepare your soul for the journey."

Moses spent his last hour blessing Israel's tribes. Then, escorted by the priest Eleazar, he began to climb Mount Nebo. Slowly he entered the cloud waiting for him. He took one step forward and turned around to look at the men, the women, and the children who were staying behind. Tears welled up in his eyes. When he reached the top of the mountain, he halted.

"You have one more minute," God announced. Then God said, "Lay down on the ground and close your eyes." Moses clutched the ground and closed his eyes. And God said, "Fold your arms over your chest." Moses did so. "Moses," said God, "now. I will take your soul myself." Then, silently, God bent over Moses and kissed him. And the soul of Moses found shelter in God's breath and was swept away into eternity.

Then God sat down and wept. "Now who will oppose evildoers? Who will speak for me and love me as Moses did? And whom will I love as well?"

God's angels and all the souls in heaven came to comfort God. "Oh Lord, why do you grieve so? In death as in life, Moses is yours. His soul will be with you forever and always."

"Always and forever!" sang the soul of Moses.

We find the classic message of this midrash by examining the moving and subtle dialogue of the most powerful hero in biblical history struggling with his own mortality, clinging to the last dregs of life, and resisting the very Divine Will he followed unsparingly. Moses is courageous and cowardly, fiercely loyal and fleeing in fear. He is transparently human. His persona and personality command our attention and draw us into the fascinating, intimate, frightening, and complex relationship he shared with YHWH – "I shall be there with you, as who I am I shall be there."[3] Moses transforms human understanding about the nature of God from the Wholly Other Remote One to Intimate Presence who promises to be there-with-us, now, accessible, and visibly active. It is to this God that Moses talks, as a friend, face to face (Exod. 33:11a; cf. Num. 14:14, Deut. 5:4, 34:10).

What does the story of Moses teach us about our own journey to the promised land of self and center? How does this inexhaustible narrative touch us anew across the expanse of millennia? What quality or capacity in Moses enables him finally to hear the voice? The wise old man and wise old woman who is Moses presents the seeker for life and life abundant with the fundamental human choice: to come face to face with our egocentric, unconscious selves in order to grow in the direction of becoming whole and free, attentive to our inner world and its workings. The blessing and burden of it all is aptly rendered through the mapping and metaphor of Moses' journey. First, however, a brief exploration into biblical prophecy will assist the reader to grasp more fully the nature of the God who so desperately desired that Moses hear.

The Prophet as Bearer of God's Pathos

In short, the prophet of Hebrew tradition is prepared to bear YHWH's pain. The depth of the inner sensitivity to God's pathos urges the prophet to unload the burden God is bearing. The prophet is guided not by what the prophet feels but by what God feels (Heschel 1962, p. 314). To the prophet, God is unmistakably real and shatteringly present. The authentic prophet is disinterested in *theories or ideas about God*; the prophet is intuitively and intimately engaged in understanding the *desires of God*. Knowledge of God is relationship with God not by analogy or induction but through encounter and consciousness.

The prophet reveals God's desire for and human capacity to engage in an "I-Thou" relationship with the intimate divine.

The wisdom of Rabbi Abraham Heschel is invaluable in pursuing the deep insights about the inner nature of prophetic life. Through the lives of the biblical prophets we gain a glimpse into the terrible beauty of such intimacy with YHWH. In the biblical view, human experience moves God, affects God, grieves God, delights and pleases God. God is intimately affected by God's creatures and partners in creation, and because of this God possesses not only intelligence and will but also pathos. Pathos is not solely an idea about God's nature but a disclosure about the kind and quality of relationship God has with God's people and indeed creation itself. Pathos – empathy and compassion – always expresses the quality of mutual relation. Empathy is a psychic process by which one puts oneself imaginatively into the situation of another in order to feel what the other feels. Humans are a perpetual concern of God, a permanently meaningful factor in the existence of God. God does not stand outside the sphere of human suffering and crisis but is intimately bound to us with "cords of compassion" (Hos. 11:4). God is stirred by our struggles and our strivings. This God seeks to understand and be understood for the sake of the covenantal love that is the unconditional and everlasting desire of YHWH.

Equally primary in the call of the prophet to turn from idolatry and evil ways is the conviction of the prophet that God is longing for our attention and relationship. The biblical prophet refutes the self-sufficiency and eternal immutability of God. God exists in a passionate state of divine attentiveness, crying out through the prophets for us to let our hearts of stone be turned to hearts of flesh (Ezek. 11:19). "God is not a point on the horizon of the mind, but is like the air [ruah] that surrounds one and by which one lives" (Heschel 1962, p. 277). Therefore, the prophet's life is one that bears God's pathos and actually stimulates and intensifies the suffering of those listening to and often resisting the prophet's message. The prophet addresses a distortion in relation. This message cuts to the quick of mediocrity and the complacency of letting things remain as they are. The prophet is God's memory amidst a people who prefer to forget.

The message the prophet is called upon to proclaim is difficult to sustain. The prophet's very life unravels the illusion that what is can endure and be called holy. The prophet gives witness to God's pain and insists that others see and feel it for what it is (Jer. 15:18). The prophet struggles and stumbles but never succumbs to despair because the Voice and the Vision illumine the prophet's soul, spiritually *and* psychically speaking. The prophetic consciousness is convinced that any darkness that broods within and burdens human experience carries the potential inbreaking of a new time: a day of the Lord, a new creation. Prophets awaken us from a general anesthesia as a way of life. They break our façades of innocence and unexamined complicity in strategies of avoidance and tactics of injustice. They call out for us to risk hearing as they hear, understanding as they do, striving for a consciousness akin to Moses. Thus, we turn our attention to mapping Moses' inner world and its workings.

Crises Create Character

The story of Moses fits into the pattern of the myths of the birth of a hero commonly found in the traditions of various ancient peoples (Campbell 1949; Freud 1939; Ginzberg 1998, pp. 245–271; Rank 1909).[4] His saga will change the course of salvation history. It is not germane to this essay to defend or refute the historicity of Moses or the strict analyses of the biblical accounting of his life and mission. It is his interior intricacies, the terrain of his struggle, the development of his consciousness, and the way he continues to live in human spirit that captures our imagination and "draws us out" (the literal meaning of the name Moses) into the watery depths of soul-making.

Moses spent the first forty years of his life in Egypt, seemingly uncertain of his roots. He was a prince in a royal Egyptian family, but the social and political milieu of his birth was one of fear. Pharaoh had ordered the murder of all newborn male infants (Exod. 1:22). While the Book of Exodus describes in detail his extraordinary infancy and his miraculous rescue in the "little ark" set adrift on the Nile, there is silence about his childhood and adolescence. Abruptly in chapter 2 we read, "One day, when Moses had grown up, he went out to his people and looked on their burdens" (Exod. 2:11). Psychologically speaking, his early development was marked by intense inner conflicts. Following Erikson's scheme of psychosocial development, Moses struggled mightily with crises in trust, doubt, guilt, and identity confusion.[5] Raised an Egyptian, he nonetheless felt a kinship with the Hebrews. Moses was caught in a conflict of cultures that enhanced his feelings of insecurity and inner turbulence. Did Moses ever realize that the Hebrew slave who nursed and cared for him was his natural mother? How did he feel toward Pharaoh's daughter, the woman who claimed him as her son? What was his conscious awareness or semiconscious yearnings about who he was and where he belonged? What was the source of his feelings of compassion toward the enslaved Hebrews and his frustration with his advantaged and royal life?

Concern for profit did not motivate the Egyptians in their undisguised brutality toward the Hebrews. Their main objective was to hinder their increase (Exod. 1:9–10; Ginzberg 1998, p. 249). Moses knew this policy but did not seek a political solution to his inner conflicts by using his power and influence to alter the system of oppression (Wiesel 1976, p. 185). Yet Moses was strangely awakened to the injustice of the burdens of the Hebrew slaves while sensing a curious and compelling kinship with them in their plight. His frustration and anger over Pharaoh's cruelty boiled up, and he aggressively lashed out and killed an Egyptian who was "beating a Hebrew" (Exod. 2:12).[6] Observing the brutal exchange instantly triggered an uncontrollable reaction in Moses.[7] Moses thought his violent deed went unnoticed until the next day when he attempted to intervene between two Hebrews fighting each other. He questioned their turning on one another only to receive the retort, "Who made you prince and judge over us? Do you mean to kill me as you killed the Egyptian" (Exod. 2:14)? The very ones he thought he was avenging in the murder of the Egyptian turned on him and threatened to expose his deadly deed. His fears multiplied; he was trapped by the truth. "Surely," Moses frets, "this thing has come to light" (Exod. 2:14b). Moses perceived no other recourse than flight from both the murder he willfully perpetrated and the betrayal by those he intended to avenge. His confusion must have been profound. "These two Jews knew. And so that man he had addressed insolently: Spare us your sermons; are you planning to kill us too? The man knew Moses' secret: that he had killed to save a Jew – and that he himself was Jewish. Otherwise he certainly would not have dared to speak so rudely to one of the Pharaoh's favorite princes" (Wiesel 1976, p. 186).

Moses faced a turning point in his growing self-realization and self-actualization. The depth of his crisis was not only about who he was biologically but who he wanted to become psychologically and socially. His flight from truth and Pharaoh's threat on his life opened his journey toward truth and the courage to face the inner enemies of his integrity. His experience of estrangement and wandering in the wilderness was a journey into his deeper character and foreshadowed the exodus he led on a grand scale for his people.

Born Again by Water: Receiving the Feminine

In the next ten verses, the classic text reveals again its ever-abundant wisdom. The man Moses, now forty, symbolically speaking, wanders uncertain and unhealed. While there are no biblical details of his interior experience, it is not a significant leap of imagination to suggest that during this season of wilderness wandering, Moses' sense of alienation, anger, self-accusation, and loneliness must have been acute and unremitting. No doubt the challenges of this new time, so different from his previous privileged life, change his priorities. His daily search to meet basic human needs opened him to the issues of survival faced by those he met along the desert way. The daily emotional and physical strains of fleeing from fear and searching for safety and security sharpened his instincts and opened his senses to reading his inner and outer environments. Far from being a purely negative experience, Moses' forced encounter with the desert was a blessing in disguise.

When Moses wandered into the land of Midian (where descendants of Abraham lived, Gen. 25:1–6), he had become a different man than the one who fled Egypt in anger and in fear. It is not by chance that Moses found his way to a well where women come to draw water (Exod. 2:15b). The women and the water are suggestive of an impending season of new birth for Moses.[8] Aggressive shepherds (an oxymoron) threaten the women by preventing them from drawing water from the well. Without hesitation or self-regard, Moses intervenes on their behalf. This time, however, no one is killed. Moses dispels the threat to the women and proceeds to assist them with their task. The text records that "Moses stood up and *helped them*, and watered their flock" (Exod. 2:17, emphasis added).

Moses' capacity for avenging anger is once again displayed. Irrespective of his own personal turmoil, he remained attentive to injustice and brutality leveled undeservedly at others. Moses acted this time, however, in a new way. Moses "stands up" to the intruders at the well and "helps" the women. While the aggressive shepherds are more in number, Moses' manliness dissuades them from hurting the women, and Moses' gentleness enables him to take the time to help them with their task. It is not beneath him or an insult to his strength to help women draw water from a well and then water their flock with them. During the period of wandering in the desert wilderness, Moses encountered his own vulnerability. Suffering from an unrestrained and volatile personality, Moses discovered, through his grief and loneliness, that he had the capacity for a gentler relationality.

Because of his action on behalf of the women, whose father was a Medianite priest, Moses was offered a safe haven in the household of Jethro. "And Moses was content to dwell with the man, and he gave Moses his daughter Zipporah" (Exod. 2:21). In the next verse, we read of the birth of Moses' son, named Gershom, meaning "I have been a sojourner in a foreign land" (Exod. 2:22). Midrash on this period in Moses' life says that "by the way he tended the sheep, God saw his fitness to be the shepherd of his people, for God never gives an exalted office to a man until he has tested him in little things" (Ginzberg 1998, p. 300). Moses settled into a healing, relational period of time spent in Midian that was one of preparation, of inner unfolding and growth. Guided by the wisdom figure Jethro, a wife and child, and the ways of shepherding, Moses now sojourns in the inner territory of reciprocal love. The authentic experience of loving is always healing. The psychological and spiritual development of Moses in Midian centers largely around his relationship with Jethro. Jethro is the wise, caring father figure who redeems the absent father of his origins and the harsh taskmaster father, Pharaoh. Jethro is a name that literally means "overflowing with excellent qualities" (ibid., p. 290). As Moses heals, he readies unaware to hear the voice waiting to encounter the depths of his soul. Scripture suggests Moses spent forty years in Midian. The symbolic length of this time is to teach us that the process of psychospiritual integration is not accomplished overnight.

It is a well-known tenet of depth psychology that human personality achieves its quest for wholeness and deep healing through the balancing of the features of masculinity and femininity within each human being. If wholeness is to be realized, albeit partially, then one must undergo the refining of uncovering, discovering, and integrating the feminine and masculine – anima and animus – dimensions of human personality.[9] John Sanford writes that a man develops his manhood not only by performing stereotypical or even archetypal feats of masculinity, but necessarily through the creative relatedness to the feminine, for without this embrace of the feminine within, masculinity becomes boorish or brutal (Sanford 1974, p. 91). Moses is a striking example of this process. The pull toward individuation arises during the Midian time, where his act of compassion toward the women results in a strong and gentle response of concerned action without violence.[10] Such behavior wins the attention of a wise man. The father and priest Jethro entrusts his daughter to Moses, and he receives a woman whom he first met at a well. Their love generates new life. As a husband and father, Moses establishes a hearth and cares for his family of choice and progeny of his own. For forty years, Moses lives into this season of integration and healing with no apparent need to remember the drama he left behind in Egypt.

Healed He Now Hears

The Midian experience is a season of inner attunement for Moses. It was a lengthy time of growth necessary for him to be able to hear the voice that would be unmistakably true, perfectly clear, and compelling. The impending encounter with depth will direct Moses to take up his destiny and continue his lifework on a new scale. The Exodus narrative speaks of YHWH who hears the groans arising from God's chosen in bondage (Exod. 12:23–24). We again confront a God who feels, hears, and remembers; a God involved in human life and history; a God who desires that creatures and creation itself exist in a "condition" of *shalom*.

God's unrelenting desire for connection and Moses' readiness to enter the threshold of his mature adulthood result in a life-altering encounter. "Moses, Moses." "Here I am." A call made and a response given without hesitation. I AM speaking in inner clarity of voice to one prepared to hear and answer, "I am here" (Exod. 3:4), and thus revealing a level of intimacy between the Divine and human unknown until Moses.[11] God reveals a mysterious availability to Moses as to no other human being (Plaut 1981, p. 406). Moses' ability to identify himself as "I am here" suggests that he successfully met the challenges of the many developmental crises posed as both opportunity and obstacles to his becoming. Symbolically, the flight into Midian and the forty years of Midian time was the exact process needed for Moses to redeem the symbolic Egypt within himself in order to be able to return to Egypt and liberate his captive kin.

As the river Nile and the well at Midian held the water of birth and rebirth for Moses, so the mountain holds the meaning and majesty of the mission time in Moses' life. Ancient midrash records, "As a magnet draws iron, even so did the holy mount draw Moses" (Ginzberg 1998, p. 415). Amid the foothills, Moses is keeping the flock of his father-in-law (Exod. 3:1). Over the years, Moses was familiar with wandering peacefully in the foothills of Mount Horeb, also known as Mount Sinai. The openness and expanse of the foothills mirrors his growing openness to and expanse of the unconscious moving up from the depth and taking Moses closer to the center of wholeness. Moses reconnects with the groans of his people and reintegrates Egypt into himself without self-recrimination or fear. This call from God is a psychospiritual inevitability for Moses. It is the coming to fruition of his lengthy intrapsychic struggle in Egypt, the terrifying terrain of his flight and wilderness wandering, and the period of preparation in Midian. Moses comes to terms with himself. The burning bush is a confirmation of the fruits of his soul-searching: individuation.[12] Moses understands the thornbush aglow as a vessel of divine vision. Under the guise of nature, the supernatural, the *Shekinah*, announces its presence and its transforming power. He hears the inward groans of his people and knows their groaning as his own.

Freed from inner conflicts that once prompted a reaction of flight, Moses stays in place, takes off his shoes, awed at the unquestioning clarity of the mountain theophany. The voice is burning with desire and deliverance. Moses engages the voice in the way Moses and God will relate from that day forth: "mouth to mouth, clearly, with no dark speech" (Num. 12:3). The authenticity and transparency of the conversation that ensues between Moses and God is *conversio*, meaning transformative dialogue. The burning bush was the invitation to arise from the foothills and enter the dialogue with Depth. How is Moses so sure that the voice is not a projection of the remnants of his untamed grandiosity? How does he know that the desire he feels and the deliverance of which he hears arises from other than his own egocentricity? He knows because "he knows."[13] Human understanding cannot fully grasp the nature and quality of such mystical experience from a purely scientific point of view. The confrontation with YHWH gives form and purpose to that which had been stirring restlessly and conflictually within him. Moses stands barefoot upon the ground trembling with the ground of all being. This first theophany emerges as a moving and vivid expression of the inner struggle of a man coming to a fullness of selfhood meeting its center and ground. The burning bush can be understood as the successful engagement of yet another developmental crisis pushing Moses into maturity with a mission. Thus, authentic dialogue flowed and a new relationship with depth was born in Moses that would endure until his death at a hundred and twenty years or, as midrash tells, even into eternity!

The Legacy of Taking Moses and God Seriously

Once Moses registers that he does indeed hear his name, a conversation ensues that plunges Moses into divinely revelatory and historically revolutionary events. God says more to Moses about who God is and how God acts than God has ever previously revealed. Moses balks and questions God (Exod. 3:11, 13). God listens to Moses express his seemingly insurmountable fears about his lack of credibility and eloquence (Exod. 4:1, 10). It is said that God urged Moses for seven days to undertake the mission (Ginzberg 1998, p. 322). Moses' resistance finally results in "God's anger kindled in Moses" (Exod. 4:13–14). While God concedes to send Moses' brother Aaron to assist Moses in the mission of liberation, the "kindling" of God's anger within Moses is the reception of the divine energy that must pulse in the heart of the prophet.

The passionate conversation – *conversio* – recorded in these biblical verses discloses an authentic dialogue where the exchange between the persons creates new understandings, attitudes, and actions that deepen relation, establish trust, deal with fears, and give birth to mutual empowerment and well being. The "I-Thou" displayed by Moses and God tells a dramatic story about human capacity for conversation with the Divine and teaches us that God refuses an "I-it" relationship with human beings. Moses is never an *object* of divine instrumentality; Moses is God's beloved who talks with God face to face. Carl Jung calls this process of dialogue and confrontation *Auseinandersetzung*. This German word literally means "taking something to pieces." It refers to the transaction that takes place when two people passionately engage one another in dialogue or negotiation. This exchange takes place with each person holding his or her ground, unafraid of the conflict. The confrontation is authentic and empathic as each comes to understand and receive the other point of view (*metanoia*). They reach mutual resolution; relationship is deepened and consciousness is born from the conflict (Stein 1998, pp. 143–144). The mutuality mediated by authentic confrontation is the stuff from which covenants are created, restored, and renewed.

This is part of the legacy bequeathed to the sons and daughters of Moses. The God of Abraham, Sarah and Hagar, Isaac and Rebecca, Jacob, Rachel, and Leah is the God who self-discloses as "I shall be there with you as who I am I shall be there with you." In being-there-with-us, as with Moses, God expects engagement, conflict, honest dialogue, and the just and healing human actions that arise from mutual empathic listening. While God is called by many names, God is what God is by virtue of God's activity, immanence, in concrete history. That is to say, one cannot really know God, in the biblical sense of knowing, until and unless one is open to experiencing God in the direct immediacy of one's own life.

There is something more here than simply giving to God various anthropomorphic attributes in order to assuage our terrifying inadequacy to grasp the Incomprehensible. What transpires between Moses and God – mouth-to-mouth, face-to-face, friend-to-friend – makes God more vulnerable to us. While Moses exhibits the appropriate awe and respect, he nonetheless talks with God and influences God through the experience of their unique relationship. God is willing to do the bidding of Moses. There is mutuality in the relationship between Moses and God that is primary, more traditional, than the dogmatic theology of an immutable and omnipotent Prime Mover and First Cause. Our obsession with naming and containing God can get in the way of the actual *conversio* God desires and needs. Moses shows us who we are meant to be.

Herein, I believe, may be the reason Irene Dugan was hesitant to permit me, her spiritual novice, to read Ira Progoff's manuscript and thus to dwell too deeply on a prophetic theology and theophany of God. Moses was eighty years old before his interior readiness enabled him to enter into the transformative conversation God desires. One's character needs to be sufficiently formed; inner disciplines need to be readied to handle the implications of the relationship. One must possess enough maturity to bear the love and the mission. In our early years of spiritual direction, Irene told me that she would let me know when I was "in my majority." She sometimes said things that I didn't quite understand but sensed I ought not pursue in the moment. When I cut my long hair at age twenty-five, she smiled broadly and noted that I had come into my majority. Again, while not fully understanding its seeming importance to Irene, I knew it was a symbolic coming of age, the dawning of a new time for me of growth, maturing, and facing the challenges of adult life. During our last conversation together, Irene age eighty-seven and me age forty-seven, she looked straight into my eyes while telling me she wanted me to "have" her class ("The Inner World and Its Workings") and to make sure that I picked up a box of her papers she left for me at the Cenacle convent. There was a pause and then she said, "It's about the legacy . . . you know, the legacy."

Irene seemed to me a blazing thornbush of sorts herself, because she bore God's pathos, stimulated discomfort with all forms of spiritual complacency, and lived the classic truth about character and crises, in light and shadow as all humans do. Ira Progoff grew to see a transparency and congruency in her and called her a wise old woman and a wise old man. The legacy is the potential of our human character to be forged through crises, which is always opportunity for growth in disguise. The power of the classic text speaks anew:

> I have set before you life and death, blessing and curse; therefore choose life that you and your descendants may live, loving the Lord your God, obeying [God's] voice, and cleaving to [God]; for that means life to you and length of days, that you may dwell in the land promised to your ancestors. (Deut. 30:19–20)

We can choose to remain uncertain of our roots, avoiding an innate drive to uncover the "more" of our existence. We can fall into forgetfulness and stop remembering that the journey to the promised land is the quest of the gift we call life. We can insist that the biblical and mystical faith of ancient Israel is beyond our capacity to grasp and encounter. We can hold our pathos at bay and fail to permit its pain to instruct us in the ways of YHWH. We can be unintegrated, inwardly multiple until deep into old age, and still be considered to have lived an apparently successful, albeit superficial, life (Stein 1998, p. 175). In forfeiting our Mosaic heritage, however, we run the risk of infidelity to the theological and depth psychological understanding of realizing the human potential that bears our own name. Each person, created in God's own image, is "the being who possesses the capacity for the infinity of absolute spiritual openness for becoming . . . who alone possesses the capacity for the eternal" (McCool 1975, p. 24). There are no shortcuts to the promised land. This classic truth and enduring mystery we learn unmistakably from Moses – the wise old man and wise old woman – and those others among us who take off their shoes.

Earth's crammed with heaven,
And every common bush afire with God;
But only [those] who see it take off [their] shoes –
The rest sit around and pluck blackberries.

— Elizabeth Barrett Browning, "Aurora Leigh"

Notes

1. Recent communication with Jon Progoff, Ira Progoff's son and executor of his estate, revealed that Ira Progoff wrote "Moses and God" in 1950 and for personal reasons never sought publication of the manuscript. I consider it both an honor and a sacred trust to have been privileged to read "Moses and God" more than twenty years ago. This essay does not contain any direct quotes or specific content from Progoff's manuscript and should be read as substantively my own work relying on the wisdom of those directly identified in the text.

2. While the Greek term *metanoia* is usually translated to mean "change of heart," its more accurate translation means a change in one's attitude and understanding. Thus, the experience of spiritual *metanoia* is best interpreted as both an intellectual or mental movement in understanding and an affective emotional experience "of the heart."

3. For a fuller discussion of the exegesis of God's name, see John Courtney Murray, *The Problem of God* (1964, pp. 6–16).

4. Selections on Moses' inner journey are reprinted with permission from Avis Clendenen, "Portrait of Promise: Moses and the Journey to Consciousness," *Journal of Psychology and Judaism*, vol. 24, no. 4 (Winter 2000) © 2001, pp. 261–274.

5. Erik Erikson charted eight stages of psychosocial development: 1) trust versus mistrust, 2) autonomy versus shame and doubt, 3) initiative versus guilt, 4) industry versus inferiority, 5) identity versus identity/role diffusion/confusion, 6) intimacy versus self-absorption/isolation, 7) generativity versus stagnation, and 8) integrity versus despair. For a detailed description of these stages see Erik Erikson in *Childhood and Society* (1950), pp. 219–234, and *Identity and the Life Cycle* (1980), pp. 54–82.

6. For an interesting midrash on this key incident, see Louis Ginzberg, *Legend of the Jews* (1998), pp. 279–282.

7. In Jungian terms, the psychologically charged moment that Moses experienced is referred to as the constellation of a complex. To have a complex constellated is to have one's buttons pushed, resulting in the exertion of a force beyond the conscious control of the person. A complex contains hidden content that holds a psychic wound. Once constellated, uncontrollable reaction often follows. Greater consciousness about and deeper integration of this material or content into the psyche results in more rapid recovery from complex-induced stimuli, and subsequently a more integrated personality. See Murray Stein in *Jung's Map of the Soul* (1998), pp. 42–45.

8. The women at the river's edge – the natural mother of Moses and his sister Miriam – who both gave Moses to the water and received him from the water, and the women at the well in Midian represent the challenge of the anima that eventually bears fruit when the more fully integrated Moses is able to call the waters of the Red Sea to part in order to save the people (Exod. 14:16–29; Ginzberg 1998, pp. 290–291). Only women participate in the saving of the infant who is hidden among the reeds in the Nile River. Later in Moses' life, it will be seven women at a well that create a crisis for his character to bloom in a new way. As Moses integrated the feminine into his character, he became strong enough to face the challenge of the Reed (Red) Sea as a saving moment for his people.

9. The anima and the animus are the archetypal images of the eternal feminine and the eternal masculine respectively. The anima is the feminine in man's unconscious that forms a link between ego-consciousness and the collective unconscious and potentially opens the way to a more integrated self. Positively, the anima makes a man nurturing and relating; negatively, she makes him moody and unreliable. The animus is the masculine in woman's unconscious that forms the link that opens her to a more integrated self. Positively, the animus brings objectivity, perseverance, and spirituality to a woman; negatively, he makes her opinionated, domineering, and argumentative. While a feminist critique of Jung's notion of the anima and animus finds them stereotypical, the essential notion of striving for deeper integration of the masculine and feminine in human personality remains a worthy psychospiritual insight.

10. True individuality is the product of the personal struggle for consciousness that Jung called the individuation process. Individuation is achieved as a by-product of the hard inner work of ego/persona facing the emotional challenges of the shadow and achieving a deeper, more balanced unity of self. Stein aptly calls the shadow "the image of ourselves that slides along behind us as we walk toward the light" (Stein 1998, p. 88).

11. The articulation "Here I am or I am here" is also attributed to Abraham (Gen. 22:1), Jacob (Gen. 46:2), and Samuel (1 Sam. 3:4). It is the passionate dialogue following the declaration that singles Moses out from the others and suggests that what unfolds between Moses and YHWH is uniquely revelatory.

12. Midrash records: "A pagan once asked a rabbi: 'Why did God choose a bush from which to appear?' He answered: 'Had He appeared in a carob tree or a sycamore, you would have asked the same question. However, it would be wrong to let you go without a reply, so I will tell you why it was a bush: to teach you that no place is devoid of God's presence, not even a lowly bush'" (Plaut 1981, p. 407).

13. There is an oft-quoted remark that Carl Jung made when asked if he believed in God. Jung is said to have replied, "I *know*. I don't need to believe, I know" (Sanford 1974, p. 96).

References

Browning, E. B. 1867. *Aurora Leigh and Other Poems*. New York: J. Miller.

Brueggemann, W. 1990. *Biblical Insight into Life and Ministry: Power, Providence and Personality*. Louisville: Westminster/John Knox Press.

Campbell, J. 1949. *The Hero with a Thousand Faces*. Princeton, N.J.: Princeton University Press.

Clendenen, A. 2000. Portrait of promise: Moses and the journey to consciousness. *Journal of Psychology and Judaism* 24(4):261–274.

Erikson, E. 1950. *Childhood and Society*. New York: W. W. Norton.

_____. 1980. *Identity and the Life Cycle*. New York: W. W. Norton.

Freud, S. 1939. *Moses and Monotheism*. New York: Alfred Knopf.

Gerstein, M. 1994. *The Shadow of a Flying Bird*. New York: Hyperion Books.

Ginzberg. L. 1998. *The Legend of the Jews*. Baltimore: The John Hopkins University Press. Originally published: Philadelphia: Jewish Publication Society of America, 1909–1938, 7 vols.

Heschel, A. 1962. *The Prophets*. New York: Harper and Row.

McCool, G., ed. 1975. *A Rahner Reader*. New York: Seabury Press.

Murray, J. C. 1964. *The Problem of God*. New Haven, Conn.: Yale University Press.

Plaut, W. G., ed. 1981. *The Torah: A Modern Commentary*. New York: Union of American Hebrew Congregations.

Rank, O. 1909. *The Myth of the Birth of the Hero*. New York: Robert Brunner.

Sanford, J. 1974. *The Man Who Wrestled with God: Light from the Old Testament on the Psychology of Individuation*. New York: Paulist Press.

Stein, M. 1998. *Jung's Map of the Soul: An Introduction*. Chicago: Open Court.

Tracy, David. 1986. *The Analogical Imagination: Christian Theology and the Culture of Pluralism*. New York: Crossroad.

Wiesel, E. 1976. *Messengers of God: Biblical Portraits and Legends*. New York: Summit Books.

Giving up the Faith –
In Order to Be Faithful

✤

Dick Westley

FOUR YEARS BEFORE SHE DIED, I WAS PRIVILEGED TO INTERVIEW
Irene Dugan for a pastoral newsletter I was editing at the time. It
was a wonderful experience filled with wise sayings so characteristic of Irene. One of her sayings from that day has had a profound
effect on me, never moving very far from my consciousness, acting as
a kind of "charter," legitimating my own meager efforts at truth telling.
Ever fearless, here are Irene's words from that interview:

> Evil in the Church arises from authoritarianism, not true "authority,"
> which says *ab audire* – I move from what I hear within me, and it is the
> truth which speaks to me. The hierarchical Church is so afraid of truth
> that it has to fabricate its own. And it says that *this* is what we have to
> live according to, and I mandate this legislation to you who don't know
> any better. They are still saying this from the Age of the Serfs. And very
> often, I am sure, the serfs had a native wisdom that would have out-
> witted them. Still there have been more horrors done in the name of
> God than this world dreams of.
>
> That is why people are raging against authority but don't know why
> they are. They just know that something is wrong, and they want out,
> and then they become violent. I think *that* is what is at the root of all
> the modern day eruptions, i.e., the corrupt authority to which we are
> subjected on every level – on *every* level. So *when I move from the truth
> that is in me I hurt no one – but I scare the whole world.*

In keeping with those words, and in memory of my friend, mentor, and spiritual director, I lovingly offer the following reflections in her memory.

Introduction

I would like to begin this reflection by citing two authors, one from our common past, the other a notable contemporary.

The first will initiate a little theological nostalgia, as I recall Aquinas's account of "faith" in *De Veritate* XIV, 1. There he says that the human intellect is normally determined by evidence, that is, by its proper object, something intelligible to the human mind. In the absence of evidence, the human mind usually withholds its assent. But, as Aquinas notes, such is not the case in matters of faith. Lacking the specification of evidence, the human intellect assents to matters of faith not on any evidence but at the command of the will. One will only "believe" if one wants to, and one wants to because of something other than rational evidence. Aquinas concludes his account in *De Veritate* with this warning: although the human intellect assents to matters of faith at the command of the will, it remains restless because of the lack of evidence, and so even though it has given its assent it continues to yearn for, pine after, and search for some rational basis for that to which it has given assent, for that in which it believes. Hence the ongoing inner tension and turmoil that accompany all but the most fundamentalistic of believers.

The contemporary author is perhaps as well known to you as Aquinas – the premier American theologian, Jack Shea. I want to share with you a thought he expressed in a talk entitled "Changing Deeply or Dying Slowly":

> You see what happens is that human persons from the deep reservoir of spirit and of the human community facing the multiple situations of their lives create institutions to respond to human needs. Create health care, create education, create religion, create government, create businesses – and *all* of these things are a combination of outer need and inner entrepreneurial "spirit" that responds to that outer need. But these creations of the human spirit have a lingering temptation. They seem to want to break loose and go off on their own. They want to become functionally autonomous, no longer connected with and serv-

ing the Spirit that created them. They not only become different, they even become alien, odd and oppressing, attempting to conquer and overcome the very Spirit that gave them birth.

Spirit has done what Spirit does – it creates. But the creation got loose, it became other than Spirit created it to be, and then turned on the human spirit for which it was created and tried to crush it. And so according to the "prophetic tradition" of the Bible we have become the victims of the work of our own hands. And so each age is called upon to assess the state of the institutions it has inherited from its ancestors and is charged with and responsible for reconnecting them to their vital source – Spirit.

Aquinas makes us mindful of the fact that the inner struggle to believe is a constant, something that marks all the days of our lives. Jack Shea makes us mindful of the fact that even the best institutions, the Catholic Church, for instance, sooner or later find themselves in need of being reconnected with Spirit. I ask the reader to keep both these thoughts in mind as we proceed to reflect on what I take to be the "ultimate" challenge for Catholics in the third millennium: giving up THE faith *in order to be faithful.*

Evidently, I Am Not Alone

When it comes to this matter of "losing the faith," I take some consolation in the fact that I am not alone. It seems to be a dynamic that is being played out in many Catholic lives these days. In his book, *American Catholic,* Charles Morris writes:

> [Today] the Church is ripped with theological dissensus. The rejection by rank-and-file Catholics of much of their Church's official teaching on sexual and personal morality has long been a staple of the daily press. But even more fundamental dogmas are losing their hold on the laity – fewer than half of the most faithful Catholics, those who attend Mass every Sunday, report that they believe in the Real Presence of Christ in the Eucharist, one of the Church's bedrock dogmas. Less well known is the fact that the clergy is more often aligned with the laity. Surveys from the mid-1980s found that fewer than 20 percent of the younger clergy believed that birth control is always wrong; fewer than

40 percent thought that homosexuality or premarital sex are always wrong. Older priests were more conforming to the official line, but not dramatically so. Almost a third of the younger clergy did *not* agree that the "Catholic church is the one, true church established by Christ," and almost no priest under forty-five believed that doubting one article of faith calls the whole of religion into question. (Morris 1997, p. 293)

Obviously, something is afoot when committed Catholics, not the nearly fallen away ones, start talking like that. How are we to account for the present situation?

What's Going On?

There are several possibilities. It could be that we are being so assimilated by our secular culture and its capitalistic consumerism that we have lost our ability to continue living as people of faith. Many in high places in the Church continue to play on that theme, and with just cause. For many of our contemporaries that is exactly what has happened. They have been, and continue to be, seduced by individualism and the constant search for greater and ever newer pleasures. They have "given up the faith" in order to better fit into our secular culture.

But there are others of us who are not at all attracted to the path our culture is taking. We do not answer but passionately reject its siren call. We resent being lumped in with the first group. It is advantageous for those in power in the Church to characterize us that way because then they don't have to take our objections seriously and can dismiss us by stereotyping us with the broad brushes of "materialism" and "hedonism." How utterly convenient for them! We are "giving up the faith" of our youth because we have "matured" in our God-relations and the old answers no longer make sense to us, because we recognize that Vatican II and our own experiences of the Spirit of God in our lives have called us to a new "Exodus," an exodus for the third millennium. In short, we are giving up the faith not to run from God and our spiritual responsibilities but in order to be more faithful to them.

Spiritual Maturity

Everyone's spiritual life begins by taking what others tell us as normative and true. There is no other way to begin the spiritual journey because there is no countervailing story available to us when we are children. But we do not remain children. In the process of living our lives, a countervailing story rises to consciousness from our own lived experience. More precisely, from our own lived experience of God. That is why Paul could write to the Corinthians: "When I was a child I used to talk like a child, think like a child, reason like a child. When I became a man I put childish ways aside" (1 Cor. 13:11).

As a matter of fact, God and God's ways are revealed to us primarily through normal everyday experiences, rather than through the esoteric and specialized experiences of the mystics, the jargon-laden discourse of the theologians, or even the authoritative proclamations of our religious leaders. When it comes to discerning "the ways of God" – if one really pays heed to one's life, experience is the best teacher.

Without doubt, life itself *is* our best teacher. Mindful Christians not only know that that is so, but *why* it is so. We know from the Judeo-Christian tradition and our own lived experience that our God is the God of life not death; that God has actually chosen to live in us, in our inmost parts; and that that divine presence at our center makes our lives authentic fonts of revelation, from which we may, if only we are so inclined, learn life's deepest truths. Indeed, as we mature, become adult and grow older, this experience-based truth becomes paramount in our lives. No longer children, we have matured to the point where we recognize that many things in our religious tradition are incompatible with the God of our experience. Being "adult" means that one has acquired an almost natural ability to discern that crap is crap no matter who says it. Thanks to the presence of God in our lives, we have access to a source of sacred truth that is independent of our religious leaders. If what they say doesn't jibe with "communally funded" adult experience, it simply lacks authority, for example, the magisterial proclamations about the immorality of contraceptive lovemaking between spouses or the impossibility of ordaining women. In the last analysis, it is the God-filled human experiences of believing people that are ultimately authoritative in their lives. *It is experience that should shape our theology, not theology our experience.*

The patron saint of that process of spiritual maturing is, I would submit to you, St. Peter. I have always had a soft spot in my heart for impetuous Peter, who, with all his faults, loved the Lord and was chosen to head the flock. Whenever he is mentioned in Scripture, his humanity shines through; he is one of us, and his spiritual journey is a pattern we all seem to follow more or less. That is what makes the text from the tenth chapter of Acts a favorite of mine:

> I begin to see how true it is that God shows no partiality. Rather, people of any nation who fear God and act uprightly are acceptable to him. This is the message he has sent to the children of Israel, the good news of peace proclaimed through Jesus Christ who is Lord of all. (Acts 10:34–36)

I cannot help but ask myself why, if the first pope finally came to see that essential truth, so few popes since have been able to accept and act on it. Raised in the Jewish tradition that Israel was God's chosen one, Peter spent most of his life with that conviction. But in trying to walk with the Lord, he came to see something that had been unthinkable before. And even this text doesn't say that he saw this something clearly. He was still struggling. "I begin to see . . . ." That is, he was beginning to have an inkling that what the institutional religious establishment has taught us all wasn't quite right. Who of us has not had that very same experience? It is comforting to know that St. Peter preceded us in this difficult experience. Acts 10 should have made Christian fundamentalism impossible, but alas not only is it possible, as we begin the third millennium it is becoming ever more virulent. Of the many things to be said against the move toward fundamentalism in our time, perhaps the most important is that it short-circuits spiritual maturity and closes one off from the revelatory dimensions of one's own life and the transforming power of the Spirit.

Second Vatican Council

About ten years after the close of Vatican II, the U.S. Catholic Conference of Bishops held a meeting of laypeople for brainstorming the role of the laity in the Church. We met in a retreat house outside Annapolis, Maryland, and Archbishop Jean Jadot, the apostolic delegate to the United States, was in attendance. We sat together at one of the meals and had a wonderful and spirited exchange, which I shall always remember most fondly though it certainly was not my finest hour. Jadot was open, caring, eager to listen and very easy to talk to. I, on the other hand, was the typical "ugly American," being somewhat pushy and determined to take this rare opportunity to give a papal nuncio a piece of my mind. The issue was joined when the conversation turned to the documents of Vatican II, which Jadot praised highly. He said they were the finest ecclesial documents ever produced by the Catholic Church. I jumped into the fray by dogmatically proclaiming that they were the worst documents ever produced by the Catholic Church. To make my case, I pointed out that they were ambiguous and anything but clear, that they read like a statement in which the liberal bishops wrote one line and the conservative bishops wrote the next. What one sentence gave, the very next sentence took away. This meant that both liberals and conservatives could interpret them to their own liking. "Church documents should at least be clear and unambiguous – is that asking too much?" I said.

Jadot did not become defensive at my outburst but remained open and gracious as the conversation went on. We never did agree. When the conversation ended, Archbishop Jadot gently added this piece of wisdom as a footnote: "Council documents are so rich that we can't plumb their depths very quickly; it will take a hundred years or more before we really grasp their meaning."

Well he was certainly right about that. Only four decades have passed since the end of the Second Vatican Council, and we are just beginning to understand the revolutionary secret at its center, a secret that significantly changes the center of gravity of the Catholic enterprise and is more severely dividing Catholics today than at any time since. This contributes mightily to the present conflicted state of the Roman Catholic Church.

The Secret of Vatican II One of the most quoted metaphors used to describe the central purpose of Vatican II is unfortunately misleading. We have all heard that Pope John XXIII called the Council to open the windows to let the air in to revitalize what had become a rather musty church. So it was natural for us to assume that the main task of the Council was to "renew the church." Without for a moment denying that the Catholic Church was, and still is, in urgent need of renewal – in Jack Shea's words, of being "reconnected with the Spirit" – that was a secondary goal, not the primary one.

As Jesus wept over Jerusalem and the plight of its people, that great lover John XXIII wept over the state of the world in which he lived. He looked out on a world in which science and technology have run amok, proceeding to their own ends without regard for the moral order or the effects they are having on people. A world in which people are ever more divided from one another, and peace seems an impossible dream. A world in which the majority live in poverty and want, saddled with unjust economic and political institutions that favor the well-off few and effectively prevent any betterment of their situation. In short, good Pope John looked out over our world, the contemporary world in which we now live. And after he had wiped away his tears, he determined to call a council, not primarily to renew the Church, but to call upon the Spirit "to renew the face of the earth," that is, to improve and humanize life for *all* the inhabitants of the "blue planet."

Pope John made clear his intentions in the talk he gave to open the Second Vatican Council. It was entitled "Humanae Salutis," which should not be translated so much as "human salvation" in the religious sense but as "human well-being" or "human flourishing" in the everyday sense. Pope John understood that at the heart of every human person is a passionate concern for the worldly well-being of oneself and one's loved ones. This is a fundamental interest of each one of us, be we believers, agnostics, or atheists. But that basic interest of all humanity is thwarted by the threat of nuclear and biological warfare, by the senseless and dangerous destruction of the ecosystem, by the corruption of human values in a technological and materialistic world, and by a world economy that does not allow the poor and marginalized to rise above a subsistence level of life.

If the goal was to change the secular world in which we live, a plan was needed, a plan in which the Church was going to play a central role. Pope John had such a plan. It can be likened to a fifteenth-century allegorical morality play, in which the actors on stage portrayed certain virtues.

Pope John's version goes something like this. In the twentieth-century scenario, believers going about their daily lives in the world are to be the actors. The audience is the rest of humanity suffering in the contemporary world. As the audience watches the actors, it will catch a glimpse of the attitudes, motivations, and goals behind actions performed on behalf of the audience. The audience will begin to resonate to the authentic human values expressed in the theodrama revealed by the lives of believers. This will empower the audience in the depths of their own experience to discern their own authentic humanity and dignity and their own true end. As that happens, a new human solidarity will be forged, a new humanity, the beginnings of a whole new world, a whole new civilization – a civilization of love. This was Pope John's dream and goal.

Of course, for the Church and its believers to be effective actors in this twentieth-century morality play, they would have to be themselves renewed, revitalized, and refocused. So Pope John had Vatican II focus on three things: (1) the type of mind, heart, and action believers would need to be effective actors in the morality play, that is, effective in building a more human future for all; (2) a program to set Christianity's house in order and to heal the scandalous divisions among Christians themselves; (3) a program among all people of good will leading to world peace, human development, and economic progress. This meant that the pope was directing the Catholic Church to address the most basic and fundamental question of any age or culture: What does it mean to be fully human? What kind of a world is required to put that goal within the reach of all, regardless of gender, race, or religion?

Just rehearsing the story of Pope John's Council is edifying and spiritually uplifting in the telling. How in the world could such a noble agenda ever become a source of anger, dissension, and division among Catholics? In order to understand the radically revolutionary and controversial nature of the Council we shall have to look a little deeper.

Christo- and Ecclesio-centric vs. Regno-centric For the past two thousand years the Christian enterprise has been governed by the last commissioning of the disciples by Jesus as recorded in the final verses of Matthew's gospel. It is the basis for the traditional understanding of evangelization.

> All power is given to me in heaven and on earth. Go, therefore, and
> teach all nations, baptizing them in the name of the Father, and of the

Son and of the Holy Spirit. Teaching them to observe all that I have commanded you. And behold, I am with you always, even unto the end of the world. (Matt. 28:18–20)

On the threshold of the third millennium, Pope John's Second Vatican Council seems to have changed that central focus of the Church's mission. The goal is no longer to convert *all* people to Christianity or Catholicism. The Christian mission still involves a conversion, but now it is a conversion of people's hearts whereby they change their lived priorities and begin putting topmost value on developing their true humanity, recognizing their authentic ultimate end, and responding to the divine presence in their lives, however the Spirit of God leads them. Our mission is to so live Kingdom values in our own lives that it will be an invitation to *all* people to do the same. Of course, for purists, that is to say, fundamentalists, this change of emphasis is unacceptable because it changes absolutely everything, and about that they are correct. However, they quickly return to their erroneous ways when they accuse the proponents of Vatican II of abandoning Christian faith in favor of some sort of humanism.

Despite the many official Vatican statements endorsing the Council, Pope John Paul II himself seems to have some grave reservations about the current change of emphasis. He worries about the impact such an interpretation of Vatican II will have on Catholic identity and evangelization, that is, on the Church's sense of mission. For two millennia Christians have operated on the premise that the Christian Church was somehow necessary in God's plan for the salvation of the world. Indeed, for centuries, the dictum "outside the Church there is no salvation" was taken quite literally, and Catholics took great comfort in knowing that they belonged to "the one true Church." That essential element in traditional Catholic identity is severely compromised, and even obliterated, by the current interpretation of Vatican II's agenda.

More specifically, Pope John Paul II raises the following objections to what a growing number of theologians say Vatican II was really all about. In their account: (1) the Church is not concerned about itself but with serving the Kingdom of God and its emergence among all the peoples of the earth; (2) it stresses Kingdom values like peace, justice, freedom, community, and religious tolerance and runs the risk of becoming totally anthropocentric, human centered, and secular; (3) it gives an account of Christian salvation that is God-centered and Kingdom-centered, not Christ-centered and Church-centered, thus reducing the essential salvific role of both Christ and his Church.

At last we come to the heart of the present conflict in the Church. If one changes the mission of the Church from that of converting everyone to Christianity/Catholicism to converting everyone to living out Kingdom values in their lives, the consequences of such a seemingly simple change are profound. One cannot change the mission of the Church without also changing one's understanding of who Jesus is, of what the role of the Church in the world is, and of what we mean by salvation. In other words, tampering with the traditional understanding of "mission" unravels the whole fabric of Catholic theology as we have known it in the first two millennia.

This can be looked upon in two ways. It can be rejected out of hand as the work of the devil and the destruction of Christian faith. Or it can be welcomed as Spirit-driven, ushering in a new and revitalized Christianity for the third millennium. As you may suspect from my remarks, I prefer to view it the second way, which is why I have likened our present situation to the Exodus story of the Old Testament and suggested that in order to be faithful we must answer the call to a new exodus from our twentieth-century faith to a new revitalized faith for the twenty-first century. It will be a journey in which we must leave the land of our childhood faith, and courageously follow the Spirit's lead to a promised land of a more mature faith for the new millennium.

Coping with Dogmatic Baggage

If we are really going to have an exodus into the new millennium, like our Jewish ancestors we are going to have to travel light, leaving some things behind we thought we could never do without. In concluding, I would like to mention a few of items from our dogmatic baggage that will have to be left behind. There are some "unbelievables" that we just cannot take with us on the journey if we are to be faithful to the Spirit.

The Catholic Religion Is the "One True" Religion

As we have seen, even St. Peter began to doubt the validity of such a triumphal claim. As we enter the third millennium it is long past time for us to follow his lead in this regard. Thanks to technology and the communication explosion of the Internet, we are at last on the threshold of "one world," the "global village." As we interact with people of other ethnic and religious backgrounds we will discover many of them to be kindred spirits, responding in their way and according to their tradition to the presence of God in their lives. We must rejoice in our spiritual kinship and not try to arrogantly convert them all to our ways and the Christian tradition. Only then can we be faithful to the God who dwells not only in us but in them as well.

"Revelation" Ended with the Death of the Last Apostle

What an affront to God to say divine revelation ceased nearly two thousand years ago and all we can do now is draw forth from that wellspring of revelation that has been put in the keeping of the Catholic Church. This is tantamount to putting the infinite God in a very tiny box of our own making. More than that, anyone who undertakes the spiritual journey in earnest is well aware from personal experience that divine revelation continues in our age. By claiming that it does not, official religions can close their minds and hearts to the ongoing revelation of the Spirit in the people. What better time than the third millennium to consign this haughty claim to the dustbin of history?

Salvation Comes *Only* Through Jesus and His Church

My junior and senior years of high school were religiously very significant. In 1943, the most significant encyclical of Pope Pius XII's pontificate appeared: *Mystici Corporis Christi,* on the "Mystical Body of Christ." To this day I remember verbatim the most revolutionary statements from that encyclical. The first proclaims the fact that laypeople living their daily lives are capable of reaching the heights of supreme holiness, which was not to be thought to be restricted to celibate priests and religious. Long before Vatican II, Pius XII gave us the charter for a truly lay spirituality:

even the fathers and mothers of families, under the impulse of God and
with His help can reach the heights of supreme holiness, which Jesus
Christ promised would never be wanting to the Church. (Pius XII, no. 17)

The second proclaims that the salvation of the world depends on
members of Christ's Church, the Mystical Body. They are, as it were,
co-redeemers with Christ.

As he hung upon the cross, Christ Jesus won for us an unending flow of
graces. It was possible for him personally and immediately to impart
these graces to man, but he wished to do so *only* through a visible
Church made up of men. (Ibid., no. 12)

Dying on the cross, he left to the Church the immense treasury of
redemption towards which she contributed nothing. But when these
graces come to be distributed not only does he share this task with his
Church, but wants it in a way to be due to her action. Deep mystery
this, subject of inexhaustible meditation, that the salvation of many
depend on the prayers and voluntary penances which the members of
the Mystical Body offer for this intention. (Ibid., no. 44)

This great encyclical introduced the phrase "offer it up" to the Catholic
lexicon and started anew the whole movement of "Catholic Action"
after the Second World War. It was simply marvelous. To this day, I
remain a Mystical Body Catholic in my soul. Surely Pius XII was correct about the role of the laity and about the fact that the work of salvation is communal. But he was most certainly wrong in seeing the
Church as the necessary intermediary between God's saving grace and
humankind. This notion slanders the gracious God of every gift and
has no place in the third millennium.

The Institutional Church Controls the Means of Salvation

According to the Baltimore Catechism, a sacrament is an outward sign,
instituted by Christ, to give grace. According to the new Roman
Catechism, "Sacraments are efficacious signs of grace, instituted by
Christ and entrusted to the Church, by which divine life is dispensed
to us."

For centuries the Catholic Church has claimed control over the very means of salvation, which it takes to be the sacramental system and which it puts squarely in the hands of the ordained. I am sure that at the beginning there must have been those who laughed at the thought, just as the Native Americans laughed at the pilgrims who "paid" them for the land because they believed that land could not be owned. Similarly, think how ludicrous it is for the institutional Church to claim ownership of the very means of salvation. Who in their right mind would ever make such a claim, and who but the most childish of Christians would ever take it seriously?

As we have now come to understand, the sacraments are not so much the source and cause of saving grace as the liturgical celebrations of believers of graces already received. Sacraments do not cause God's gifts or grace, they celebrate them. At least, such will be the universal Catholic understanding in the third millennium.

The Arrogance of Absolute Claims by the Magisterium

The latter half of the twentieth century has seen the Magisterium (the Teaching Church) claim, if not always in words at least by its actions, an absolute position in the faith-life of everyday Catholics (the Believing Church). By doing so, it has broken with an ancient tradition of the Church, captured in the theological dictum: "The Teaching Church can only proclaim authoritatively what the Believing Church already believes."

In the past, the Magisterium was always balanced by and in some ways held accountable to the *consensus fidelium*, the communally funded truth arising from the spirituality and lived experience of believing people. It is only recently, in our day, that the Magisterium has arbitrarily chosen to completely disregard the *consensus fidelium*, making itself the sole source of Catholic orthodoxy and practice. The Magisterium now acts as though it can teach anything it wants regardless of what the Spirit of God is revealing in the lived experience of the people. This is exactly what happened with Paul VI's *Humanae Vitae*, his famous encyclical on birth control. The Magisterium is neither absolute nor unconditioned – and so in the third millennium we shall see the Catholic Magisterium reined in and its proper counterbalancing relation with the *consensus fidelium* restored.

Priesthood – Paul's Letter to the Hebrews

In Christianity there is only one High Priest, Jesus the Lord. The rest of us participate in that one priesthood. All of us participate in it through baptism and by becoming part of the priestly people. In addition, some of us are ordained in Holy Orders.

In his letter to the Hebrews, Paul speaks of the ordained priest as mediator between God and humankind, and consequently that has become the standard understanding among us. However, because God's people need no mediators with God since God dwells in them, we now need a better description of ordained priesthood. God and humankind are so intimately related there is no room or need for a mediator. To keep ordained priesthood relevant, we shall have to rethink it in the third millennium.

Conclusion

I would be remiss were I to pass over in silence the most dramatic and important source of conflict today, what we might call "the Jesus question." What say we of Jesus of Nazareth? Strange as it may seem, Catholics are now divided on this question, which is really two questions. Is Jesus God, the Second Person of the Trinity, or is Jesus divine in some other sense that applies also to us? Is Jesus the *only* Son of God, above all others, in whose name alone salvation comes to humankind?

There is much work to be done on this issue. It is already underway. It may take a whole millennium before it is settled. Until it is settled, we must possess our souls in patience, knowing that however that theological controversy turns out, Jesus is for us the model of what it means to live a human life according to God's plan and open to the Spirit. Whatever one's theology, we are all called to do likewise.

O God, Maker and Nurturer of us all, we ask your special grace to soften our hearts and open our Spirits to the Church you are even now molding in our midst. Much in us still resists, still looks to the past as our only access to truth, as if you were to be found "back there." Enlighten us as to where your truth is to be found, and give us the strength and courage to pick up and leave the Church of our youth and joyfully go forth to meet you where you are. As Abraham left his homeland at your call, so we ask the grace to answer that same call in these difficult times. Father, free us of religion. Fill us with faith. Make us ready for the future. We ask you this, in the name of Jesus, our Brother, the Risen and totally open to the Spirit One. Amen.

References

Morris, Charles. 1997. *American Catholic: The Saints and Sinners Who Built America's Most Powerful Church*. New York: Random House.

Pius XII. 1943. *Mystici Corporis Christi*. Encyclical of Pope Pius XII, June 29, 1943. N.C.W.C. edition.

Shea, Jack. 1997. Changing deeply or dying slowly. The Hillenbrand Institute, Old St. Patrick's Parish, Chicago, Illinois, May 29, 1997.

Living the Spiritual Life with Authority

✺

Robert J. Bueter, SJ

Preface

IRENE DUGAN WAS A SPIRITUAL AUTHORITY AS WELL AS A TRUE friend. She was deeply invested in people, making time and space in her life for a wide variety of friends. Yet she was magisterial in her manner and approach to people and situations. One example after another of this attitude or bearing came forth as the people creating this book gathered to plan its shape and substance. Irene, while visiting one of us at home, learned that a child of the family was troubled and not acting well. She wasted little time in taking him aside and talking to him; his behavior improved. He later remarked simply to his parents, "She had authority." Amid recalled wonder at her zest for life – from the arts to restaurants – at her intuition and vision, at her depth of spiritual understanding, there was the nodding recognition that through it all Irene was an authoritative teacher.

I experienced Irene's authoritativeness in two ways that have brought me to this project and chapter. The first was in the early days of my ministry, the troubled days after Vatican II. Community life is always difficult for the strong and personable, and it was especially so in those controversial times. Irene, as the extremely gifted individual that she was, experienced markedly the dynamics and difficulties such a person encounters in living the common life of a religious order. The inner spirit of one's religious order can be deadened or hindered, on occasion, by the atmosphere of the community one happens to be living in. With her usual directness, Irene told me once, "Remember, your community is not just those you are living with." Her point was that your true community is not the particular group but the sources of life that you can find in other members of your religious order as well as in others outside its membership proper. In our meeting to plan this volume, we could sense the community of spirit that Irene had helped each one of us find. It cut across gender, generation, and genius.

"Go to your studies" Irene also told me in the early days of my ministry when I complained to her that the day-to-day teaching and coaching (and, later, administering) was leaving an intellectual void in my life. I never forgot that advice, although it was not until I was in my fifties that I finally got a sabbatical year to pull it all together and launch the doctoral program that provided the opportunity to reflect and to write what follows.

Irene was a good authority, and good authority is important to have and keep.

Problems with Authority

We all rely on authority; to do so is a very human characteristic. We may check the reviews before visiting a restaurant or choosing a movie; there are rating guides for everything from automobiles to Web sites; we call upon this or that friend whose advice has been helpful in the past. But when it comes to questions of morality and values or social convictions and religious concerns these days, it is hard to find authoritative guides either in society or church.

In matters civic, the presidential election of 2000 took respect for secular authority to a new low in the United States, even questioning the authority of the highest court in the land. The naked partisanship of both camps, mouthing principles while grabbing for power, impugned the authority of all the traditional sources one might look to: the lawmakers, the lawyers, the justices, and the writers of fact and opinion. It all smacked of posturing and platitudes, if not downright prejudice, and there seemed to be no permanent principles or positions purposely thought through.

The 2000 election continued an unfortunate trend that began with Richard M. Nixon and the cover-up after the Watergate break-in. That disrespect for secular authority intensified with William Jefferson Clinton and the tawdry tale of his Oval Office and telephone trysts with Monica Lewinsky. And as though those shenanigans were not bad enough, they led to further revelations of incriminating moments in the personal lives of such illustrious icons as Franklin D. Roosevelt, Lyndon Baines Johnson, and John F. Kennedy.

In matters religious, Roman Catholics in the United States have come a long way since the 1950s, during which there seemed to be great confidence and trust in everything about the American Church, whose authority was not an issue. There was even a little smugness about it back then, the entire American Church seen as being "on top of the world." That was Charles R. Morris's description, in *American Catholic*, of the American Church at its zenith in the 1950s with Father John Corridan "On the Waterfront," Bishop Fulton Sheen on television, and JFK on the campaign trail to the White House. For American Catholics, church attendance was robust, divorce was unthinkable, and parishes had schools with nuns and rectories with several curates – all of whom were lionized and listened to by a trusting people.

The decline in Church authority began just before Watergate with the publication of *Humanae Vitae* and the widespread dissent that it occasioned. That lack of trust has intensified and is currently playing itself out in the ongoing controversy over such Vatican initiatives as *Ex Corde Ecclesiae* and *Dominus Jesus*. Here, too, historical writing is thrusting allegations and assertions from the past into our current evaluation of church authorities such as Pius IX and Pius XII. Noted Catholic author Gary Wills has penned a scathing criticism of papal authority, *Papal Sin*, accusing successive papacies from the nineteenth century to the current pontificate of building "structures of deceit" to uphold shaky teaching and tactics in the areas of anti-Semitism, contraception, and clerical ordination.

More pointedly and poignantly, the current dismay over pedophilia cases in the clergy, the continuing discussion of the sexual orientation of the clergy, the decline in the numbers of vocations, as well as complaints about homilies and liturgy from the right as well as the left – all this makes it clear that dissatisfaction with authority figures in American Roman Catholicism is much more than opinion about the current practice or past performance of distant authorities. They are concerns laid before everyone, at the altar, in the pulpit, and at home in discussions around the family dinner table.

Teaching with Authority

Is there any authority you can rely on? Why bother with authority? As I mentioned at the beginning, Irene Dugan was noteworthy because of her magisterial manner. We are reminded of the gospel that Jesus "taught as one having authority." In Roman Catholic theology, we cannot run far from the affirmations that Jesus is the definitive Word of God, a special revelation of who God is and what we are to do with our lives. In our faith, we know that Jesus taught with authority because he is the ultimate authority on the will of his Father, and he is authoritatively "the way, the truth, and the life." The full theological expression and philosophical articulation of our Trinitarian faith took centuries to develop, and this chapter will conclude with the implications of that Trinitarian faith for authority. But we begin not with the Jesus of faith, but the Jesus of history.

The Jesus of history, as he is recovered by ongoing scriptural scholarship, is a figure who poses a challenge to the positions of current controversialists. The Jesus of history does not fit conveniently into the presumptions and current assumptions of the two major groups in current controversy.

In matters civic, the sides are taken in what has been termed the "culture war," in the phrase and analysis of Gertrude Himmelfarb (author of several articles and, most recently, *One Nation, Two Cultures*) among others. This "war" pits those of a more traditional and conservative bent (the "right") against those of a more liberationist or liberal point of view (the "left"). While the current prosperity of what some are terming a new "gilded age" has blunted the supposed conflict, anyone following the battle over dimpled chads realizes that the war goes on – and with vigor.

In matters religious, and specifically American Catholic, I call this the "ideological divide" in the American Church. There are manifest liberal and conservative schools of thought in the Church that are fairly hardened into what might be thought of as "camps." A primer on the subject would be Morris's *American Catholic,* a book that illustrates the divide by describing two parishes that are direct opposites of one another and yet both very popular and dynamic. The ideological divide is quickly seen in the mail solicitations that come from one side or the other on this or that issue, from right-to-life and natural family planning groups on the one hand to those lining up for the annual protest at the School of the Americas or urging a wider role for women in the Church on the other hand. To get on the mailing lists, just make a nominal donation to your favorite nun, Mother Angelica, on the one side and the president of NETWORK on the other. If you prefer to follow the war only on a weekly basis, subscribe to the *Wanderer* and the *National Catholic Register* on the one hand (the right hand) and the *National Catholic Reporter* and *America* on the other (the left hand). If you want to join in, there is the Newman Society or the Catholic Theological Society of America.

The Domestication of Jesus

The facile appropriation of a partial or limited vision of Jesus has long been a concern of mine, starting back in the countercultural zeitgeist of the revolutionary 1960s. My first awareness that scholarship and partisanship are rarely in concert began in summer school in 1968. A young nun – in full habit, mind you – stood up in Marcel van Caster's class and stated rather dramatically, in the spirit of the times, "Then you could say that Jesus was the first of the social revolutionaries?" The noted Belgian catechist paused, stared down at her over his glasses, and replied, with only a slight accent, "Yah, yah, you could say that, but that would not be the Gospel. And we must preach the Gospel." From that time forward, I have been on the watch for any attempt to read current social analysis and modern political commentary back into the mouth of the historical Jesus and out of the gospel into a rhetorical justification for this or that work or point of view.

In the instance of the "social revolutionary" Jesus, we have to address a general point and a specific point. In *Jesus and the Revolutionaries,* Oscar Cullman noted the generic difficulty of bringing any portrait of Jesus to the present time: "First of all I would point to the exceptional difficulty of the problem . . . that Jesus' attitude *cannot be simply* transferred in to our time . . . . A type of 'adaptation' to the present is therefore necessary. But exactly here the problems begin" (1970, P. 52).

The problem leads to overly facile statements such as the young nun's. But, to be more specific, she did have in part a point. The historical Jesus, as he emerges from the current round of scholarship in what is being called the "third quest" for the historical Jesus, is hardly a supporter of the status quo. That is where the temptation to make him into a social revolutionary gets its impetus. The gospel text will not allow what John P. Meier, in his ongoing *A Marginal Jew* (two volumes published with a third in preparation), calls the "domestication" of Jesus.

The young nun, like so many of us in the revival and renewal associated with John XXIII's calling of the Second Vatican Council, may have been reacting to the smugness that Morris pointed to in the American Church entering the 1960s. Religion, like all human endeavors, can suffer from a loss of its force. As a religion grows, such as the post–World War II Catholic Church in America, it can become bland and mundane. As Meier points out, this is a perennial problem, very American, at least since the time of Thomas Jefferson:

> [There is] one popular portrait of the historical Jesus often found in literature today: Jesus was a kindhearted rabbi who preached gentleness and love in the spirit of Rabbi Hillel. This domestication of a strange first-century marginal Jew bears a curious resemblance to the domestication of Jesus undertaken by Thomas Jefferson some two centuries ago. (1994, p. 1045)

Meier has been acknowledged in the review literature as the most thorough and centrist of those writing in this third quest, and for Catholics, especially of a more traditional bent, his work bears the imprimatur of the late Cardinal John O'Connor's censor. Meier and others have come to some definite conclusions about the historical figure who "taught with authority." Jesus was hardly domestic:

> In contrast, a first-century Jew who presents himself as the eschatological prophet of the imminent arrival of God's kingdom, a kingdom that the prophet makes present and effective by miracles reminiscent of Elijah and Elisha, is not so instantly relevant and usable. Yet, for better or for worse, this strange marginal Jew, this eschatological prophet and miracle-worker, is the historical Jesus retrievable by modern historical methods applied soberly to the data. (Ibid.)

In the current tension with authority in the Church, there would seem to be a prima facie case here that Jesus would be on the side of the dissenters. An itinerant Jewish preacher who takes liberties with traditional teachings, while at the same time being very liberal in his table fellowship with male sinners and females from across a wide spectrum of respectability, hardly seems Roman curia material. There is indeed much here to encourage those who see Jesus as a figure of change and opposition to authority, namely, "his association with the religious and social 'lowlife' of Palestine [and] his prophetic critique of external religious observances that ignore or strangle the inner spirit of religion" (Meier 1991, p. 199). Certainly the renewal of the 1960s and 1970s was an attempt to encourage an inner spiritual growth. And that was good.

But not all that has been brought forward in the attempts at renewal is necessarily right, especially concerning the social revolutionary Jesus. That school of thought is still strong and strongly critical of authority. Leonardo Boff, a liberation theologian who had his problems with the Vatican's Congregation for the Doctrine of the Faith (CDF), has this to say recently about the CDF's *Dominus Jesus*:

> Worse yet is the fact that there is no mention of the poor. For Jesus and the New Testament, the poor are not just one theme amongst many. The poor are the starting point where one begins to understand the Gospel as the Good News of liberation . . . . There is no resonance of this announcement of liberty and compassion to be found in this hopeless Vatican document . . . . The centrality of the message of Jesus is to be found in unconditional love and in the poor, and not in the ideological discussion put together in the Cardinal's document.[1]

Meier provides the following, which counters Leonardo Boff: "[T]he historical Jesus is not easily co-opted for programs of political revolution either. Compared with the classical prophets of Israel, the historical Jesus is remarkably silent on many of the burning social and political issues of his day" (1991, p. 199). While from this point of view, Meier criticizes "liberation theology" in particular, of which Boff is a spokesman and for which our young nun was a precursor, he hastens to add quickly that "the usefulness of the historical Jesus to theology" is that he keeps us honest "by refusing to fit into the boxes we create for him" (ibid.). The historical Jesus is "equally offensive to right and left wings . . . . Properly understood, the historical Jesus is a bulwark against the reduction of Christian faith . . . to 'relevant' ideology of any stripe" (ibid., p. 200).

I wonder if Ralph McInerny is listening. His *What Went Wrong with Vatican II: The Catholic Crisis Explained* is not a question but a statement. What went wrong is dissent:

> To accept Vatican II is to accept what the council says about the Magisterium and the Catholic's obligation to obey it. As we will soon see, public and sustained rejection of the Magisterium and of this clear teaching of Vatican II – largely by dissenting theologians – has caused and sustained the crisis in the Church . . . . For dissenting theologians to have asserted their dubious authority against that of the Vicar of Christ is a scandal of the first magnitude. (1998, p. 150)

McInerny and his attitude toward the teaching authority of the Church is an example of how the conservative side of the ideological divide emphasizes papal authority, what John O'Malley, SJ, recently termed the "papalization" of the church (2000, p. 8). This is what I call a "run-to-Rome" attitude for conceptually tight, logically consistent, and absolutely certain answers to everything from altar girls to women's ordination. In this view, the historical Jesus is reduced to the gospel texts in which leadership of the Church is passed to Peter and membership in the Kingdom is limited to carrying out directives from his successors and the papal bureaucracy. When the superior general of the Jesuit order, Father Peter-Hans Kolvenbach, was asked just a few years ago about Rome and the American Church, he stated: "Such a nervous church! A priest says this or a bishop does that, and a fax machine lights up in Rome." Then he paused, smiled, and added: "But there are so many faxes, they do not know what to do."

The historical Jesus, we must remind ourselves, challenges the rigid digging in on both sides of the divide. This is the motivation for what I write here. While my role as an administrator limited my intellectual pursuits, it has forced upon me a centrist mentality. I call it the "manager's eye," and it develops from being in authority and having to make decisions.

To be a successful administrator, you must deal with everyone and every point of view. You must come up with policies and plans that will cover in a comprehensive way the widely differing attitudes and opinions that are present in the organization. You are under a constant barrage from activists and protagonists who call you on the phone, write you letters, or take you aside in social functions, saying, "Don't you agree, Father . . . ." The sides are there, and Meier is correct in cautioning both of them to be very careful in enlisting the historical Jesus and Scripture for their side. As van Caster admonished, "We must preach the gospel." The Office of Readings for December 23 has a wonderful statement from a treatise by Saint Hippolytus:

> There is only one God, brethren, and we learn about him only from Sacred Scripture. It is therefore our duty to become acquainted with what Scripture proclaims and to investigate its teachings thoroughly. We should believe them in the sense that the Father wills, thinking of the Son in the way the Father wills, and accepting the teaching he wills to give us with regard to the Holy Spirit. Sacred Scripture is God's gift to us and it should be understood in the way that he intends: we should not do violence to it by interpreting it according to our own preconceived ideas.

Authority is the major issue in the current divide, so I propose in the rest of this chapter to review what the New Testament has to say about the authority of Jesus. We will examine all the texts, forty-two of them in the Revised Standard Version, in which the word authority occurs.[2]

While this is an exhaustive search of the New Testament instances of the word *authority* in one translation, I do not pretend to exhaust the subject of authority in the Church. Back in 1966, with the official approvals of an imprimatur, a nihil obstat, and an imprimi potest, the late John L. McKenzie, SJ, with the Second Vatican Council still in session, wrote *Authority in the Church*, a fairly thorough review of the New Testament on the subject. In the first chapter of that book, the noted scholar describes its scope:

> Our area of investigation is the idea of Church authority in the New Testament; and our first step is to study the texts in which the idea of

authority and other ideas closely related to authority appear. I have tried to make this collection complete as far as the idea of authority directly is concerned; and this includes passages in which the use of authority in the apostolic Church is described. After the texts have been examined, we can attempt a synthesis. (1966, p. 21)

If it took this great scholar an entire book to exhaust the subject, our survey here sets a more modest goal.

My contention is that the New Testament, on its face and in a non-technical reading, first gives aid and comfort to those annoyed if not alarmed by the acrimony of the current combatants. In addition, it will suggest that the combatants in the culture war and in the arguments across the ideological divide may have missed something. That something, as I will present it at the end, is the source of Jesus' authority. That source, I would hope, might lead those on either side of the divide, in the spirit of the Cenacle that Irene Dugan modeled so well, to tranquil meditation and mediation rather than tempestuous argument and accusation.

Chapter and Verse on Authority

There are gospel and other New Testament texts that deal with authority in general, and we will start there before turning to those dealing with the authority of Jesus in particular. The first is when Jesus heals the centurion's son:

> But the centurion answered him, "Lord, I am not worthy to have you come under my roof; but only say the word, and my servant will be healed. For I am a man under authority, with soldiers under me; and I say to one, 'Go,' and he goes, and to another, 'Come,' and he comes, and to my slave, 'Do this,' and he does it." When Jesus heard him, he marveled, and said to those who followed him, "Truly, I say to you, not even in Israel have I found such faith." (Matt. 8:8–10)

Jesus is not distanced from this Roman centurion because of his secular authority, and despite what we know from the Bible and other sources about the tensions with Roman authority, in Luke's version of the story (Luke 7:2–9), the Jewish bystanders even put in a good word for *this* Roman because of his good deeds. There is little hint elsewhere in the New Testament that in and of itself authority is suspect.[3]

In fact, authority is presented as very foundational, much like a primordial cosmological force, in the Pauline literature and Jude:

> See to it that no one makes a prey of you by philosophy and empty deceit, according to human tradition, according to the elemental spirits of the universe, and not according to Christ. For in him the whole fulness of deity dwells bodily, and you have come to fulness of life in him, who is the head of all rule and authority. (Col. 2:8–10)

> For this reason . . . I do not cease to give thanks for you, remembering you in my prayers . . . that you may know what is the hope to which he has called you which he accomplished in Christ when he raised him from the dead and made him sit at his right hand in the heavenly places far above all rule and authority and power and dominion, and above every name that is named, not only in this age but also in that which is to come. (Eph. 1:15–16, 18, 20–21)

> Then comes the end, when he delivers the kingdom to God the Father after destroying every rule and every authority and power. (1 Cor. 15:24)

> Now to him . . . be glory, majesty, dominion, and authority, before all time and now and forever. Amen. (Jude v. 24)

In these texts, authority is much more than simply a given; there is respect and reverence for authority as part of the very foundation of the highest things.

In the light of this foundational view of authority, it is not surprising to find direct New Testament testimony that authority *is* a good thing in and of itself. Paul urges Titus: "Remind them to be submissive to rulers and authorities . . ." (Titus 3:1). And the Second Letter of Peter tells us that to "despise authority" puts you among the "unrighteous" who will be "under punishment" on the "day of judgment" (2 Pet. 2:9).

Far from suspect, his authority is what the Apostle Paul is at pains to have recognized in his churches. Even his conversion emphasizes authority. He is on a different mission, but he is still an *authorized* minister. As we read in Acts:

> Ananias answered, "Lord, I have heard from many about this man, how much evil he has done to thy saints at Jerusalem; and here he has authority from the chief priests to bind all who call upon thy name." But the Lord said to him, "Go, for he is a chosen instrument of mine to carry my name before the Gentiles and kings and the sons of Israel . . . ." Then he rose and was baptized, and took food and was strengthened. (Acts 9:13–15, 18b–19a)[4]

Paul, using the language of "boast," remained adamant that he had authority from Jesus himself ("our authority, which the Lord gave" – 2 Cor. 10:8),[5] and Paul does not hesitate to press his authority (although the word is never used) "to his face," referring to his confrontation with Peter and the other apostles in what we now term the first ecumenical council of Jerusalem (Gal. 2:11). Paul also urges Titus to use his authority: "Declare these things; exhort and reprove with all authority. Let no one disregard you" (Titus 2:15). Joining Paul in demanding an authoritative response to his position in the church is the author of the Third Letter of John who complains: "I have written something to the church; but Diotrephes, who likes to put himself first, does not acknowledge my authority" (3 John 9). Authority, far from being suspect in itself, is necessary for mission, and Paul and others do not hesitate to claim it.

But Jesus' authority is broader than mere authorization for ministry. Jesus, as Meier has emphasized, has an authority that manifests itself in its power over demons and disease. The comment concerning Jesus' teaching "with authority" in the first chapter of Mark's gospel is not merely about the power of Jesus' words. That statement does summarize the reaction to Jesus' teaching, but it also introduces the rest of the chapter in which Jesus performs his first exorcism and heals many in the crowd that had gathered:

> And they went into Capernaum; and immediately on the sabbath he entered the synagogue and taught. And they were astonished at his teaching, for he taught them as one who had authority, and not as the

scribes. And immediately there was in their synagogue a man with an unclean spirit . . . . But Jesus rebuked him, saying, "Be silent, and come out of him!" And the unclean spirit . . . came out of him. And they were all amazed, so that they questioned among themselves, saying, "What is this? A new teaching! With authority he commands even the unclean spirits, and they obey him . . . ." That evening, at sundown, they brought to him all who were sick or possessed with demons . . . . And he healed many who were sick with various diseases, and cast out many demons. (Mark 1:21–23, 25, 27, 32–34)

Jesus not only has authority in himself to heal sickness and cast out demons, he passes that authority on to his followers, authorizing them to do the same. In all three synoptics, when Jesus calls the twelve together and commissions them, he gives them "authority" not only to teach and preach but to cast out demons and cure diseases (Matt. 10:1, Mark 6:7).[6] Luke adds the commission of seventy, an account which in typical Lucan fashion adds a little more story and a lot more personality to this bestowal of authority:

The seventy returned with joy, saying, "Lord, even the demons are subject to us in your name!" And he said to them, "I saw Satan fall like lightning from heaven. Behold, I have given you authority to tread upon serpents and scorpions, and over all the power of the enemy; and nothing shall hurt you." (Luke 10:17–19)

If Jesus as a radical teacher and an unsettling prophet of reform seems clothed in revolutionary garb, these texts we have just reviewed might tempt those of a more conservative view to find him a new set of clothes, ones much more comfortable with a respect for authority.

Authority is a given, it is very foundational, it is essential for mission, and it stands out in Jesus and his disciples. But there is much more to note. Jesus' authority over demons and disease and his transmission of that authority to his followers provoke a confrontation with the Jewish leaders.

All three synoptics report the confrontation (Luke 20:1–8; Mark 11:27–33; Matt. 21:23–27); here is Matthew's version:

And when he entered the temple, the chief priests and the elders of the people came up to him as he was teaching, and said, "By what authority are you doing these things, and who gave you this authority?" Jesus answered them, "I also will ask you a question; and if you tell me the answer, then I also will tell you by what authority I do these things. The baptism of John, whence was it? From heaven or from men?" And they argued with one another, "If we say, 'From heaven,' he will say to us, 'Why then did you not believe him?' But if we say, 'From men,' we are afraid of the multitude; for all hold that John was a prophet." So they answered Jesus, "We do not know." And he said to them, "Neither will I tell you by what authority I do these things." (Matt. 21:23–27)

The conflict is about much more than healings and exorcisms. Jesus claims the power to forgive sins. The stakes in the confrontation have been escalated to a higher level, and now there is mention of blasphemy. Again all three synoptics have the episode (Luke 5:18–26; Mark 2:3–12; Matt. 9:2–8); here again is Matthew:

And behold, they brought to him a paralytic, lying on his bed; and when Jesus saw their faith he said to the paralytic, "Take heart, my son; your sins are forgiven." And behold, some of the scribes said to themselves, "This man is blaspheming." But Jesus, knowing their thoughts, said, "Why do you think evil in your hearts? For which is easier, to say, 'Your sins are forgiven,' or to say, 'Rise and walk?' But that you may know that the Son of man has authority on earth to forgive sins" – he then said to the paralytic – "Rise, take up your bed and go home." And he rose and went home. When the crowds saw it, they were afraid, and they glorified God, who had given such authority to men. (Matt. 9:2–8)

Since the authorities are fearful of Jesus, they put in motion the plans that ultimately lead to his death.

The Scope of Jesus' Authority

Meier emphasizes that it was the historical reality of Jesus that led to his death. Jesus as Meier described him earlier – eschatological, miraculous, taking liberty with the law and with custom – collides with the authorities because he was a direct threat to their authority. That much from history.

As we move to the early church's theological conclusions about Jesus, in the light of his resurrection and the early church's Spirit-filled communal reflection on the Jesus they now experience as Lord, the scope of Jesus' authority is revealed in terms that rightly should have terrified the Jewish authorities. Christ's commissioning of the church at the end of the gospel of Matthew is in fact a statement by the early church that their authority is a thing of the past:

> Now the eleven disciples went to Galilee, to the mountain to which Jesus had directed them. And when they saw him they worshipped him; but some doubted. And Jesus came and said to them, "All authority in heaven and on earth has been given to me. Go therefore and make disciples of all nations, baptizing them in the name of the Father and of the Son and of the Holy Spirit, teaching them to observe all that I have commanded you; and lo, I am with you always, to the close of the age." (Matt. 28:16–20)

This is clearly authority at an unprecedented and lofty level, relying no longer just on the historical Jesus but on his acceptance as Lord by the church. The commission recalls the opening of Luke's narrative where the devil tempts Jesus by the offer of just such authority: "To you I will give all this authority" (Luke 4:5). The text of Matthew theologically recalls the bold and sweeping language of the classic Kingdom locus in Daniel: "And to him was given dominion and glory and kingdom, that all peoples, nations, and languages should serve him; his dominion is an everlasting dominion, which shall not pass away, and his kingdom one that shall not be destroyed" (Dan. 7:14). And, as Revelation reminds us, that Kingdom is about authority: "And I heard a loud voice in heaven, saying, 'Now the salvation and the power and the kingdom our God and the authority of his Christ have come . . .'" (Rev. 12:10).

To fully understand such authority, we turn for the first time to the gospel of John. So far in non-gospel New Testament writings, it might be said that we have dealt with the phenomenon of authority, and in the synoptics with the historical Jesus' authority. With John (and grace notes from Matthew and Luke as just quoted), we move past the historical Jesus to the Jesus of faith.

The Source of Authority in John

John, too, notes the tension with the authorities in his seventh and twelfth chapters, but in keeping with his gospel, he is less concerned with the fact of that conflict but rather more interested in theological or analytical reflection on the uniqueness of Jesus' authority.[8]

As John sees it, the authority of Jesus does not stand out because of its actions (healings and exorcisms) and not just because it produces confrontation with the authorities. Rather, Jesus' authority points beyond himself to his relationship with the Father. With the Nicene Creed in hand, after centuries of theological wrangling and outright schism, we have the Trinitarian formulation to put a precise theology on what John's gospel was pointing to. Jesus' authority comes from his Father:

> "I can do nothing on my own authority; as I hear, I judge; and my judgment is just, because I seek not my own will but the will of him who sent me." (John 5:30)

So Jesus answered them,

> "My teaching is not mine, but his who sent me; if any man's will is to do his will, he shall know whether the teaching is from God or whether I am speaking on my own authority. He who speaks on his own authority seeks his own glory; but he who seeks the glory of him who sent him is true, and in him there is no falsehood." (John 7:16–18)

Beyond demons and disease and beyond conflict with the religious leaders, the authority of Jesus is even beyond the cosmological order – it reaches to a life beyond death:

> "Truly, truly, I say to you, the hour is coming, and now is, when the dead will hear the voice of the Son of God, and those who hear will live. For as the Father has life in himself, so he has granted the Son also to have life in himself, and has given him authority to execute judgment, because he is the Son of man." (John 5:25–27)

The historical Christ only makes in terms of his redemptive death and Resurrection:

> So Jesus said, "When you have lifted up the Son of man, then you will know that I am he, and that I do nothing on my own authority but speak thus as the Father taught me. And he who sent me is with me; he has not left me alone, for I always do what is pleasing to him." As he spoke thus, many believed in him. (John 8:28–30)

And his Kingdom is clearly beyond history and can only be understood fully at the end of when Christ completes the work of salvation:

> "He who rejects me and does not receive my sayings has a judge; the word that I have spoken will be his judge on the last day. For I have not spoken on my own authority; the Father who sent me has himself given me commandment what to say and what to speak. And I know that his commandment is eternal life. What I say, therefore, I say as the Father has bidden me." (John 12:48–50)

And the completion of that work will involve all three Persons of the Trinity, the Father as source, the Son as hearer, and the Spirit as illuminator:

> "I have yet many things to say to you, but you cannot bear them now. When the Spirit of truth comes, he will guide you into all the truth; for he will not speak on his own authority, but whatever he hears he will speak, and he will declare to you the things that are to come. He will glorify me, for he will take what is mine and declare it to you. All that the Father has is mine; therefore I said the he will take what is mine and declare it to you." (John 16:12–15)

The Texts, a Text, and a Word

This is certainly theological high ground in John, and it will take centuries of theological argument and philosophical articulation to work out the Nicene formulation. Through it all, the Father as source of all authority will be affirmed; authority proceeds from him and he is dependent on no one. As John has Jesus tell his followers the day of the Ascension: "It is not for you to know times or seasons which the Father has fixed by his own authority" (Acts 1:7). The texts in concert lead to a later Trinitarian formulation, but in their sheer enumeration they are compelling in stressing that only the Father has authority in himself and it is in Jesus only because of his relationship to the Father.

All well and good; but there remains one jarring text on authority that we have not addressed. It is from St. Paul, and it is stated with his usual bluntness. In an essay in honor of one of the great women of the recent past, who "had authority," it is a most troubling text: "Let a woman learn in silence with all submissiveness. I permit no woman to teach or to have authority over men; she is to keep silent . . . . Yet woman will be saved through bearing children, if she continues in faith and love and holiness, with modesty" (1 Tim. 2:11–12, 15).

There is no escaping here a male-dominated culture and Paul's acculturation to it, what we would identify as male chauvinism today. I see no way of salvaging this text from the savaging that it often faces.[9] Because of this text, there are some questions to be addressed: Must the entire array of texts we have just cited from John be attributed merely to a male-dominated culture that Paul's text testifies to? Or is there something to be said substantively for Jesus' predilection for address-ing God as "Abba" ("my own dear Father," in Meier's rendering)? Is it not very clear and emphatic that authority is not about focusing on Jesus, but about focusing on the Father, where Jesus would authorita-tively point us?

I think, for reasons the historical Irene Dugan would appreciate, we can blush at Paul's chauvinism without ignoring Jesus' authoritative teaching about his relationship to his Father. Jesus' authority was not simply in the strength of his teaching or of his miraculous deeds, it was also in his revelation of his experience of a relationship that lay behind and beyond his authority. And in that revelation, he used the word *Abba* ("my own dear Father") to describe the other term of that relationship.

This word, following Meier, comes uncontrovertibly from Jesus' mouth. Meier is adamant in opposing what he calls "advocacy exegetes" who would try to banish Father-language from Jesus' mouth in reference to his Father. "If it cannot be established as the more prob-able hypothesis that Jesus did use father-language of God, I suggest the criteria of historicity be abandoned along with the quest as a whole" (Meier 1994, p. 359). From our current concerns and issues, as I have stressed throughout this chapter, we cannot simply choose to ignore or downplay that the Jesus of history chose to express the source of his Kingdom and authority to his relationship to a father figure. The Roman liturgy buttresses that assertion in the fact that all of its collects (opening prayers) are addressed to the Father; so, too, is the structure of the Church's Eucharistic prayers, all addressed to the Father through Jesus. We follow here the old theological adage, *lex orandi est lex credendi* (literally, "the law of praying is the law of believing," or more fully, your prayer manifests your belief). Our chauvinist St. Paul always has the Father preceding Jesus in his opening salutation of his letters.

In the End

We have taken a long look at authority in the New Testament, for I think it gives us a comprehensive and challenging vantage point from which to address, in the spirit of Irene Dugan, the arguments and accusations of both sides in the current ideological divide in American Catholicism. I have outlined – for further meditation and, it is to be hoped, mediation – the caricature that each side has made either of the historical Jesus or the Jesus of faith. These caricatures domesticate Jesus and loose the full force and fury of his historicity, on the one hand, and the depth and development of his revelation, on the other.

The right, for its part, has locked into an intellectualism and absolutism that looks for a certainty grounded completely in rationality and conceptual allegiance to external directives. But the historical Kingdom proclaimed by our "marginal Jew" invites an individual to a personal choice that will radically change thought patterns just as it challenges conceptions.

The left, for its part, has more in common (it is my summary judgment) with current postmodern skepticism of all authority and foundational thinking than it does with sound theology concerning the Jesus of faith. Postmodernism acknowledges no outside authority other than its own canons. Those canons are challenged by Jesus' clear and extensive claim to a relationship with his beloved and dear Father.

Here at the end is something that Irene Dugan would urge on all of us: speak from the depths of your center and heart in relationship to your highest authority, whatever you call it. From the calmness of that center and relationship – and not from the storm of your raging emotions or from the chill of your logical thoughts – you will then speak with authority and the truth will continue to set us all free of our cultural limitations and ideological litmus tests.

Notes

1. From an Internet translation by Michael Seifert.

2. An old-fashioned concordance can take you there, but in today's world of computerized search engines, it is possible for almost any student to call up a complete listing of the relevant texts. My "engine" is the compact disk edition of *The Teachings of Pope John II* (Harmony Media, Inc.), which includes the text of the Revised Standard Version (Catholic edition), long my favorite translation upon the recommendation of the late John L. McKenzie, SJ – to cite my authority.

3. There is only one set of texts using the word *authority* that put qualifications on authority, and John L. McKenzie's prize-winning book, *Authority in the Church,* relied heavily on them, linking them to Jesus' example of feet-washing at the Last Supper. The three texts are the episode concerning the sons of Zebedee, James and John, and their request for places of honor in the Kingdom (Mark 10, Matthew 20, and the moral of the story without mention of James and John in Luke 22). In the vanguard of the liberal critique of authority, regnant in the 1960s and 1970s, McKenzie gives much shorter shrift to the other thirty-nine passages from the New Testament that are the subject of this chapter's analysis.

4. See also Acts 26:9–11.

5. See also 2 Corinthians 11 and 13.

6. In Luke 9:1, "power and authority."

7. We pass over in discrete silence the much more puzzling citations of Revelations that refer to the authority of "the beast" (Rev. 13:2–4), of "the ten kings" as well as the beast (Rev. 17:2–4), and of "another angel" (Rev. 18).

8. Here are the two passages: "Nevertheless many even of the authorities believed in him, but for fear of the Pharisees they did not confess it, lest they should be put out of the synagogue" (John 12:42). "Some of the people of Jerusalem therefore said, 'Is not this the man whom they seek to kill? And here he is, speaking openly, and they nothing to him! Can it be that the authorities really know that this is the Christ?'" (John 7:25, 26).

9. Paul's other statement about submissive wives (the required marital text of the Roman rite before its recent renewal) can be defended in its wider context and somewhat saved, perhaps, but not without argument.

References

Cullman, Oscar. 1970. *Jesus and the Revolutionaries*. New York: Harper and Row.

Himmelfarb, Gertrude. 1999. *One Nation, Two Cultures*. New York: Alfred A. Knopf.

McInerny, Ralph M. 1998. *What Went Wrong with Vatican II: The Catholic Crisis Explained*. Manchester, N.H.: Sophia Institute Press.

McKenzie, John L. 1966. *Authority in the Church*. New York: Sheed and Ward.

Meier, John B. 1991. *A Marginal Jew: Rethinking the Historical Jesus*. Vol. 1: The Roots of the Problem and the Person. New York: Doubleday

_____. 1994. *A Marginal Jew: Rethinking the Historical Jesus*. Vol. 2: Mentor, Message, and Miracles. New York: Doubleday.

Morris, Charles R. 1997. *American Catholic: The Saints and Sinners Who Built America's Most Powerful Church*. New York: Random House.

O'Malley, John W. 2000. The millenium and the papalization of Catholicism. *America* 182/12:8.

Wills, Gary. 2000. *Papal Sin*. New York: Doubleday.

From Generation to Generation: Passing on a Legacy of Hope

Bruce Wellems, CMF

Irene the Spiritual Director

FOR MANY YEARS, I HAD SPOKEN WITH IRENE REGULARLY IN spiritual direction. She offered life lessons and insights that kept me on my feet at the most critical turning points in life, both in ministry and personally. She taught me how to be a priest, how to serve, and to recognize there is only one high priest, Jesus. She began the work with me, reflecting with me, patiently. She asked questions, but forced no answers. Sometimes there were no answers. One time, when I thought I had learned all I needed to, she invited me to sit back down and reconsider. Gently, but with a firm hand, Irene cultivated a special knowledge that she said everyone has written on their hearts. She taught that each person has a mission in this life. She did not let egos or human agendas interfere with the knowledge that God's love is in each person, and that God simply does love us.

Irene's sessions with me led me toward a realization that the poor, the really poor, that is, the exploited, the abused, the neglected, the rejected, the imprisoned – the ones who love in their poverty – are the ones with whom I would want to form a relationship because they would keep me alive in a mission of true spiritual reflection and service.

Irene sought ways to meet with the people I was fortunate enough to come to know. They were the youth who are at risk. I was attracted to them by younger brothers and sisters concerned about the survival of their older siblings. I was invited to serve youths at risk by others who also cared and were searching for a way to guide the youths to make better decisions and live happy lives, ones with opportunities. I responded. The response offered me an opportunity to love and be loved, one of the fundamental rights about which Irene often spoke. Irene responded to what was in me and wanted to direct this experience to another level. It took time. She once asked, "I bet you are glad you know me?" All I could do was breathe a sigh of relief and say, "You know I am glad."

Irene looked for honesty, and confronting anything that detracted from the work of being honest. She asked me constantly to take time to reflect, write in a journal, and respond to the inner life. "Stay to the task at hand," she would remind, "there was no time to waste in idle thought that served only to lower self-esteem and breed self-doubt about the mission."

As Irene listened to and came to know the youths in the neighborhood, she invited them to her residence on Fullerton Parkway in Chicago. I was concerned she might not fit in with the group, but she told me to tell them we would have pizza and Coca-Cola. She was not worried they would not come. A couple of weeks later, we sponsored a session at the Fullerton Cenacle Retreat House. About thirteen young men and one young woman attended. Many were in a gang, and all had experienced a more difficult life than I knew. All wanted new life. To her dying day, this group was one of Irene's constant works. In fact, she planned sessions beyond her dying day, an indication of how much she valued and loved the youths at risk.

The Reflection Group

In the fall of 1996, Sister Irene began meeting with a group of teenage boys, age 14–19, on a monthly basis. Later, when she was diagnosed with pancreatic cancer, she maintained her scheduled meetings with the group, guiding youth at risk through reflections on how to live, covering a broad range of topics including how to be responsible at home, facing life when you don't have a parent at home, trying to stay out of gang violence, understanding sex, staying away from drugs, and getting an education. The eighty-seven-year-old nun was direct, sincere, and loving with these young men, and that is perhaps why there was excellent attendance. One seventeen-year-old was asked, after a session, why he listened to Irene, and he said simply, "She has authority." The group grew quickly from five to about twenty and consisted of high school dropouts as well as students who attended school (Whitney Young High School, Kennedy High School, Daley Community College), most involved in gangs, a few not.

Irene invited the young people to write at one of the sessions. When she asked them to imagine asking for a job and to write a resume that included their dreams, their education, and what they like to read, here's how one gang member responded:

> The kind of job I would like to do now is to sell stuff, or take any job that is open. My dream is to become a lawyer. I'm out of school right now, I finished up to my second year of high school, but I want to finish school maybe to go to an alternative school or school program. I attend a monthly meeting at the Cenacle Retreat House to learn how to make my life better. I like to read about action, or books about peoples' lives.

Arriving one Sunday in late June for our monthly meeting, we found Sister Irene in bed. She lay in a semicomatose state, mouth gaping open, close to death. We stood in stunned silence as we were left alone with the sister who had accompanied us in so many discussions. The ten teenagers had no idea she was so sick. Only a few weeks earlier they had prepared a banquet of barbecue, a special Mexican rice drink, horchata, and guacamole salad with her. She had stayed with them for four hours.

They all stood in a far corner of the room, respectfully watching in frightened silence. I said to the young men, "Well, guys, today's meeting is about death. You see how a person dies. If you live a life of peace, you will die a peaceful death, as Irene is doing right now." We gathered around closer to Irene, and one of them began to cry. Another reached for a tissue and offered it to him. We prayed together: "Thank you, Lord, for the wisdom we learned from this holy person, thank you for the love she gave to us . . . ." Suddenly, she opened her eyes. A sparkle of life was still alive in her eyes. Irene spoke to them. She then looked at each young man around her bed. These were the young people she loved, and they responded with much respect. Even in her death she was directing these young men regarding life.

Then each teenager touched her hand and arm. Each one said a few words and goodbye. This was one death that was different from the many deaths they had experienced among their friends. They stood in quiet vigilance outside. Sister Irene died several hours later.

Arriving home, the young men were stunned. They walked the street for a few hours, wandering and wondering in small groups. Others went home and told their parents. A few days later, they gathered again to carry the coffin to the wake, attend the funeral mass, and finally to accompany Sister Irene's coffin to the cemetery. They were the last ones to leave the graveside that day. The whole time they asked questions about death and the meaning of life. One young man recalled how Irene had considered herself "wafted" into life and thought the meetings should continue in a room we dedicated "the Waft," a small room that now gathers reading books and material to continue education endeavors and job searches, but most of all, reflection.

Educating the Mind and Heart: The Right to Be Loved

One afternoon, shortly after Irene's death, I gathered together with all of the youths. I would never have imagined what was about to transpire. The young men who knew Irene asked to meet not monthly but weekly in the Waft. We set up a meeting on a weeknight, and for fifty weeks straight we met. Twenty usually attended, with an average age of eighteen. Bolstered by their commitment and enthusiasm, and following a full year of weekly meetings, we opened an alternative high school and named it the Sister Irene Dugan Institute.

A large crowd of people, including Mayor Richard M. Daley, School Board President Gery Chico, Chicago Public School CEO Paul Vallas, Police Superintendent Terry Hillard, numerous politicians, business leaders, Chicago Park District leaders, Department of Human Services directors, teachers, ministers, parents, friends and students gathered August 27, 1998, to attend the ribbon cutting for the grand opening of the Sister Irene Dugan Alternative High School, as well as to participate in the Peace March sponsored by C.A.P.S. Together they demonstrated how much they cared and how important it was, and anyone who attended could not help but be touched by what they saw.

When it opened, twenty-five students attended the school Monday through Friday from 3 P.M. to 9 P.M. The following are some quotes from those associated with the new school:

Michael Caudillo, Head Teacher: "This is the brightest group of math students I have taught in seven years."

Commander Folliard, Ninth District: "Serious crime is down 85 percent recently – we have three additional tactical units in the area, but most important, everyone is working together to address the issue of violence."

Student at Irene Dugan Alternative High School: "The school is taking away my street life. I don't have time to do what I did before."

The alternative school and the Peace March of August 27 are part of a larger effort taking place to educate our young people. The parish is proud to be a part of a coalition of neighborhood schools and agencies dialoguing and planning strategies to educate every youth who desires education. The Peace and Education Coalition has since opened a second alternative high school just a few blocks away and continues to pursue opportunities to serve at-risk youth.

As Sister Irene had explained to the prospective teenage students: "You have a right to be fed when you are a baby, you have a right to be clothed and taken care of . . . so you have a right to be loved." The right to be loved has driven our public school principals, parish staff, and teachers in this Back of the Yards neighborhood to care for the youths currently not being cared for in the educational system.

Today: Reflection "Irene Style"

Weekly reflection sessions continue in the Waft. Almost every youth in the neighborhood now is aware of the meeting. They come as they are called, and behind it all is a spirit of Irene guiding the discussion, the spiritual direction. Greg Michie, a pastoral colleague who has been with the group since Irene's death, asks, "Can we push these guys a bit more towards the choices they must make?" Oscar Contreras, an adult from East Los Angeles and a former gang member offers, "I can call in some friends to provide some motivational talks." I sense the need to maintain the contact and encouragement. All of these responses have to do with how Irene formed relationships and encouraged reflection, self-knowledge, and an awareness of God's life.

Frank: A Lesson of Hope

If you take the word *listen* and rearrange the letters, it spells silent. To really hear the stories of our young people, we have to be silent and listen. We have published *Reflections: Young Men in Back of the Yards Look at Their Lives*, a journal of the reflections the youths have written. Frank is but one of many stories needing to be told so that this and future generations of children have hope. The following is an excerpt from Frank's story in his own words:

I was born and raised on the South Side of Chicago. As a child, all I remember is watching all my uncles' gang-bang, party, and do drugs. We all lived under one roof: me, my mom, my sister, uncles, aunts, grandma, and grandpa – everybody was in that crib. I was the only boy my mother had. My father? Who knows? [He] pulled up when I was born. [My Mom], she didn't want to raise us in Pilsen, where my uncles grew up, so we moved to the Back of the Yards. But I guess she didn't know any better, because wherever you go, it's all the same sh – , just a different gang.

By the time I was thirteen years old, I was already smoking weed, drinking beer, and learning how to bag up cocaine. By the time I was in the seventh grade, my girlfriend was pregnant, and I was already hanging in a bar. I really thought I was cool. I remember the first time the owner told me I couldn't be in the bar. My boy Stony and a few others pulled the owner aside and had a few words with him. After that, I was allowed in there all the time.

At sixteen, my lady was going on our third child. I had been in and out of the Audy home [the Cook County Juvenile Detention Center]. I starting witnessing my friends get shot, stabbed, and murdered. One time, I was standing in front of my house when I heard a gunshot come from the back. I ran back there and all I saw was a little boy getting out of a parked Blazer, crying. I asked him, "What happened? What's wrong?" He kept crying, pointing inside the truck. So I looked in there, and it was one of my boys, who had blown his brains out in front of his little brother. I never knew why he did it. His little brother said it was something to do with the gang.

So I started to grow up. I've witnessed so many of my friends that have gotten shot dead in front of my face, dying in my arms. I've also seen one of my boy's own sister get shot, laying there helpless, dying, while the f – ing cops and medical help just stood around asking questions instead of rushing her to the hospital.

I've gotten shot two times. I've gotten stabbed two times, and plenty of times I got jumped. But there will always be these two occasions that will make me wonder if it was really worth it. One time I was walking, carrying my first child in my arms, and alongside me was a lady pushing a stroller, walking the opposite way. Everything happened so fast. A truck passed and started shooting at me. When I got up, I checked to see that my son was okay. Then I noticed that a few feet away the stroller was halfway off the curb. The lady was lying in the middle of the street with two bullets to the back of the head. So because of me being a gangbanger, I almost got my son killed, and there is a little girl out there who will grow up without a mother.

Another time, I was talking to one of my boys as he was double-parked. A van passed by doing a drive-by and shot my friend in the head. All I wanted to do at that moment was go and kill somebody. But I had to go to my friend's house and tell his mom. We went to the hospital together [and] they let me go in the room with her. As her son lay there hooked up to a bunch of machines, his head all swelled up and unconscious, he had tears coming down his eyes as if he knew. A doctor walked in and said, "I'm sorry, but he's not going to make it." That's when the real hard part came watching the mom break down to her knees, crying and screaming, "Why!?" That really made me think. Would I want to put my mom through that?

Now I know why people would put a gun to their head and pull the trigger. Because they think there's no other way out. But there is, and I thank God I lived long enough to find out. (Michie 2001, pp. 10–11)

In listening to Frank, one falls silent. It is almost beyond comprehension that one so young can endure such brutality and manage to find his way from despair to hope.

The Legacy

I remain in company with those committed to at-risk youth, who understand the urgency to listen and reach out to them with alternatives before they experience what Frank describes as simply a way of life in the "hood." Sister Irene Dugan's work with all of us – adults and teens alike – provided a new avenue of hope. The school that bears her name is a community effort to change a "hood" culture marked by the blood and bodies of young people to a neighborhood where boys and girls can actually grow up to be the leaders of a new society. The sixty young men and woman who today attend the two Sister Irene Dugan Alternative High Schools have all faced tremendous challenges at a very early age. Drugs, gangs, violence, guns, poverty are all part of the fabric of their everyday lives. Each one is a drop-out from some other school for anywhere from six months to four years. Most are now or have been on parole for some type of crime. Most of them remain gang members who risk reprisal for choosing to go outside of their hood and cross into a rival gang's territory to attend the alternative school. All of them want to be *former* gang members and know that their best hope for realizing this dream is an education and a job. Twenty-eight adolescents and young adults have realized the dream of a high school diploma; eight more graduated in June 2002.

Since we began this coalition effort and opened the Dugan School, the neighborhood crime rate and homicides have reduced dramatically. In the year 2000, only one homicide was reported in the immediate area of the school. An ongoing community coalition of leaders from the schools, businesses, churches, and other agencies meet once a month to strategize on reducing violence and providing health care, adequate nutrition, child care, and restoring safety and security to the neighborhood. Local businesses participate with the school in mentoring and job placement. Thus the Sister Irene Dugan Alternative High School is a small operation – thirty students and five full-time staff – dealing with a very big problem.

Reflection times "Irene style" are part of the holistic curriculum of the school day. In addition, neighborhood teens, even elementary school children, "waft" into the weekly evening reflection and conversation sessions. Life skills are being honed through listening, silence, and love. If you take the word *listen* and rearrange the letters, it spells the silent, powerful, and life-changing embrace of love, which gives us all hope for a better future.

Reference

Michie, Gregory, ed. 2001. *Reflections: Young Men in Back of the Yards Look at Their Lives.* Photographs by Antonio Perez. Chicago: Santa Cruz Press.

Contributors

✥

Mary Ann Bergfeld, RSM, MFA, has been teaching film study and courses in the humanities for over thirty years. A member of the Institute of the Sisters of Mercy of the Americas and associate professor of humanities at Saint Xavier University in Chicago, Sister Bergfeld specializes in film theory and criticism. She has a history of involvement with the National Endowment for the Arts and the National Association of Media Educators, and has been active in the Film Center for the Art Institute and Screen Educators Society in Chicago. She continues to contribute to the contemporary critique of cinema.

Robert J. Bueter is a priest of the Society of Jesus and currently pursuing a directed research doctorate in the humanities through the Union Institute of Cincinnati. Rev. Bueter is assistant to the president of Loyola Academy in Wilmette, Illinois, and has a long history in administrative leadership in Catholic secondary education, serving as immediate past president of Lexington Catholic High School in Kentucky and past principal of St. Ignatius College Prep in Chicago.

Avis Clendenen, D.Min., Ph.D., is a pastoral theologian specializing in teaching and writing in the area of applied theology with an emphasis on psycho-spiritual development. She is presently professor of religious studies at Saint Xavier University, Chicago. Dr. Clendenen is the co-author, with Dr. Troy Martin, of *Forgiveness: Finding Freedom Through Reconciliation* (Crossroad Publishing Co., 2001). She is also completing Sister Irene Dugan's unfinished manuscript under the title of "Love Is All Around in Disguise: Meditations for Spiritual Seekers."

Michael Cooper is a Jesuit priest with a doctorate in Ignatian spirituality from the Institut Catholique in Paris. From 1979 to 1986, he combined teaching at Xavier University in Cincinnati with ministry training of spiritual directors at the Jesuit Renewal Center. From 1986 to 1998, Dr. Cooper was a faculty member in the Department of Theology and the Institute of Pastoral Studies at Loyola University, Chicago. Presently, he is the assistant to the president for University Ministry and director of the Center for Catholic-Jewish Studies at Saint Leo University near Tampa, Florida.

Irene Dugan (b. 1909, d. 1997), a Religious of the Cenacle and Honorary Doctor of Humane Letters, was a pioneer in applying the insights of depth psychology to Ignatian spirituality with specific attention to gender differences in psycho-spiritual development. A leader of renewal in religious life following the Second Vatican Council, Sister Dugan, in the traditions of the Religious of the Cenacle, took initiative in developing spiritual growth opportunities for the laity and throughout her ministerial career provided spiritual guidance and sustenance to scores of people on their journey to a spirituality in depth.

Joyce Kemp, r.c., Ph.D., is on the ministry staff of the Cenacle Retreat House and Spirituality Center in Warrenville, Illinois, where she is a spiritual director and retreat and workshop facilitator and heads the program planning and marketing teams. Trained by the late Sister Irene Dugan, r.c., and Dr. Ira Progoff, Sister Kemp is a Progoff Intensive Journal workshop leader. She holds a doctoral degree from the Union Institute in religion and applied spirituality and is the author of *The Spiritual Path of Caryll Houselander* (Paulist Press, 2001).

Jane Madejczyk, OSF, M.A., M.B.A., is a Wheaton Franciscan who holds graduate degrees from the University of Pennsylvania and Northwestern University's Kellogg Graduate School of Management. She is currently senior vice president of Mission Services for Wheaton Franciscan Services, Inc., a multistate healthcare and shelter system. She has cultivated a background in fine arts and spiritual direction.

Murray Stein, Ph.D., studied at Yale University, the C. G. Jung Institute, Zurich, and the University of Chicago. He has been a training analyst for over twenty years and currently teaches at the C. G. Jung Institute of Chicago and maintains a private practice. His numerous publications include *Practicing Wholeness* (1966), *Transformation: Emergence of the Self* (1998), and the authoritative edited collection, *Jungian Analysis* (second edition, 1995). Dr. Stein is president of the International Association for Analytical Psychology.

Bruce Wellems, CMF, D.Min., a priest of the Claretian Missionary Community, is pastor of Holy Cross/IHM Parish in Chicago. Rev. Wellems has worked in the Back of the Yards neighborhood on the near southwest side of Chicago among immigrant families since 1990 and has been devoted to increasing the quality of life, education, and job training for Hispanic youth. Influenced by Sister Irene Dugan and with the assistance of city leaders, he founded the Sister Irene Dugan Institute, an alternative high school for youth at risk, ages 14–21, sponsored by the Chicago Public Schools.

Dick Westley, Ph.D., Professor Emeritus of Philosophy, has recently retired from a forty-two-year teaching career, mostly at Loyola University, Chicago. He is the author of nine books, including *When It's Right to Die: Conflicting Voices – Difficult Choices* (1994), *Good Things Happen: Experiencing "Community" in Small Groups* (1992), *A Theology of Presence: A Search for Meaning in the American Catholic Experience* (1988), and the Catholic Book Award recipient, *Morality and Its Beyond* (1984). Still active at Loyola University's Institute for Pastoral Studies, Dr. Westley teaches and lectures widely on a post–Vatican II vision of the church and its mission.

Margaret Zulaski, OSF, Psy.D., is a Wheaton Franciscan and a clinical psychologist employing the insights of depth psychology in her work with clients. In addition to a leadership role in her religious congregation, Dr. Zulaski has a private practice in Arlington Heights, Illinois. She is a candidate-in-training at the C.G. Jung Institute Analyst Training Program in Chicago.

Index